# Practical Lessons in Hypnotism

# Practical Lessons in Hypnotism

**WILLIAM WESLEY COOK**

COSIMOCLASSICS

NEW YORK

**Practical Lessons in Hypnotism**
Cover © 2007 Cosimo, Inc.

For information, address:

Cosimo, P.O. Box 416
Old Chelsea Station
New York, NY 10113-0416

or visit our website at:
www.cosimobooks.com

*Practical Lessons in Hypnotism* was originally published in 1901.

Cover design by www.kerndesign.net

ISBN: 978-1-60206-140-8

Personal magnetism has always been
an important factor in private and in
state negotiations, and he who can exert
the greatest hypnotic influence over the others
interested in a transaction is likely
to prove the most successful.

—from *Practical Lessons in Hypnotism*
(Chapter XX, "Hypnotism in Business and Society")

## AUTHOR'S PREFACE.

This book has been written for those who are anxious to know the truth concerning hypnotism and who desire to learn the best methods of hypnotic practice. It is written in plain language for intellectual people, and all its statements are absolute facts and its illustrations are ac*ual occurrences. Nothing has been exaggerated and the sensational has been strictly avoided; for the truth of hypnotism is more wonderful than the fruits of imagination.

The reader is asked to dismiss the thought that hypnotism belongs to the field of legerdemain or sleight of hand; for that is far from the truth. It is a natural science, dealing with mental and physical actions; and the exercise of its power is the result of a natural endowment which all are capable of developing.

Those who study hypnotism and become acquainted with its laws and phenomena cannot help but realize the great benefits to be obtaii ed from it in social, intellectual and business life. It broadens the scope of thought and banishes from the mind false notions of "the mysterious relationship of soul and body." It helps to destroy bigotry and superstition and to establish truth.

From the pages of this book many facts may be gleaned that will explain the power of the mind over the body that has become such an important factor in the treatment of disease. Many hundreds of thousands of people, realizing the great benefits to be derived from the exercise of "faith" or will power, have completely discarded the use of all material substances when endeavoring to cure their bodily ailments; and to the influence of what is in reality hypnotic suggestion they trust their lives.

A celebrated medical writer once said: "It is the mystery surrounding the use of poisonous drugs that prompts human beings to blindly swallow whatever their physicians administer, and as knowledge increases, this mystery is being swept away." The philosophic mind cannot realize how poisons, with inherent characteristics to destroy life, can be physiologically utilized in restoring health, and consequently many thinking persons have joined the Christian Scientists, Faith Curists, and various other organizations opposed to medical treatment.

All revolutions are early characterized by extreme actions; and it is inevitable that both of the extreme factions that are so antagonistic in their views concerning the treatment of disease, shall finally unite upon the golden medium of truth. Proper foods, pure air, pure water, and very many harmless remedies may be judiciously administered with wonderful benefit in the treatment of disease; and when used in conjunction with "faith" or "mental healing," which are hypnotic suggestions, results may often be obtained that are little short of miraculous. Let these facts be realized by those who depend upon the use of drugs and those who discard the use of all material substances; then the ideal practice of medicine may be scientifically established. The proper study of hypnotism will hasten such a consummation, which the author devoutly hopes to realize.

There is nothing trifling in the science of hypnotism. Its truths, like the truths of all other sciences, are simple and easily understood; but it is their simplicity that renders them of such great value to all mankind.

Knowledge in any branch of science may be used for frivolous amusement or questionable purposes; and hypnotism is no exception. But it is sincerely desired that those who read this book, will read it for the good that they can acquire—the good that a knowledge of hypnotism always brings to those who possess it and the good its power enables them to extend to others.

DR. WM. WESLEY COOK.

Evanston,
        Chicago, Ill.

# TABLE OF CONTENTS.

## CHAPTER I.
### PHILOSOPHY OF HYPNOTISM.

## CHAPTER II.
### QUALIFICATIONS OF A HYPNOTIST.

## CHAPTER III.
### QUALIFICATIONS OF A SUBJECT.

## CHAPTER VIII.
### CLAIRVOYANCE.

## CHAPTER IX.
### SELF-HYPNOTISM—AUTO-SUGGESTION.

## CHAPTER X.
### ACCIDENTAL DEVELOPMENT OF HYPNOTIC POWER.

## CHAPTER XI.
### THE HYPNOTIST'S SECRET.

## CHAPTER XII.
### DEVELOPING A SUBJECT.

# INTRODUCTION.

Hypnotism is the most practical science of the age. It enters into our everyday life, and confers advantages that cannot be acquired through any other medium. Its practice is no longer a mere pastime for amusement and sensation; as professional men of the highest standing now recognize its value and seek to profit by its benefits; and scientists regard it as a natural power, for ages kept dormant, but apparently destined to perform an active part in the welfare and development of future generations.

To study hypnotism is like unfathoming the hidden mysteries of magic and human miracles and making them matters of absolute knowledge. Its possibilities are almost boundless and are interwoven with every phase of human life, and its powers are largely responsible for the successful terminations of modern business and social undertakings.

It does not require years of study to become a hypnotist, for this great blessing to mankind is a natural endowment possessed by practically everyone and capable of being developed by all who will devote to its study the patience and energy always so necessary for the development of natural talents.

The reward is great that follows the persistent study of hypnotism; for it is a science that bestows upon its devotees a power that seems almost super-human.  It overawes everyone who witnesses its indisputable facts and its marvelous manifestations. It overthrows the theories of judges and philosophers and theologians, and shakes the faith of material scientists in their preconceived opinions.  It sup-plants the physician and the surgeon and cures the afflicted and deformed whom  they  pronounced beyond the hope of recovery.  It breaks the chains of demoralizing and destructive habits.  It comforts the sorrowing and brings peace of mind to those distracted by the perplexities of life.  It abolishes periods of time and extents of distance.  It makes the lame to walk and  strengthens the weak, and causes the raving maniac to become docile as a little babe.  It checks the hand of death and snatches almost from the grave the grim destroyer's victims. It loosens the tongue of the stammerer, overcomes the self-consciousness of the backward and tempers the impetuosity of the rash enthusiast.  To mankind, in every walk of life, it is a blessing—leading his inmost thoughts to higher and nobler things; devel-oping his powers to plan and to execute and giving him social, financial and intellectual eminence among his fellow-men.  All this, and more, is hypnotism.

It does not require years of study to become a

hypnotist, although an expert can become such only through constant practice, such as is necessary to insure proficiency in any art.

Every intellectual person may exercise hypnotic power, in a greater or less degree, without regard to previous education or the established habits of life. In fact, hypnotic power is a natural endowment, capable of being developed by all who will devote to its study proper patience, energy and persistency.

The possibilities of hypnotism are almost boundless and its influence is connected with every successful undertaking of life; for which reasons we can enter upon its study with enthusiasm and a determination to develop to the fullest our latent ability.

There is no restriction upon the acquisition of hypnotic knowledge; its blessings belong to all who desire them and are willing to strive to secure them; and these blessings are of such a character that when once experienced they become absolutely essential to our enjoyment of life.

At the commencement of this twentieth century the practical utility of the science of hypnotism is universally recognized. Thousands are eagerly seeking to learn its principles and laws, that they may reap the benefits of its powers. Business men are almost unconsciously becoming practical hypnotists; lawyers are realizing that hypnotic power is the secret of success; ministers and public speakers are swaying their audiences according to the laws of hypnotism; while physicians and professors of medicine are

openly advocating and employing "suggestive therapeutics" as their most effective aid in curing disease.

Prejudice, bigotry, avariciousness and narrow-
minded sophistry have until lately succeeded in
smothering the great science of hypnotism. Men
who were bold enough to make known the marvelous
nature of the hypnotic power they were able to manifest, were denounced as wizards, charlatans, imposters and mountebanks. But now the tables are
turned. Those who were formerly denounced are
now regarded as scientific investigators; and the
doctrines they taught are being eagerly learned by
the most noted scientists. What was held up for
ridicule is now regarded as a dignified science. What
was attributed to evil machinations is now regarded
as one of the greatest of blessings to the human race.

Hypnotism has triumphed. It occupies the position of a dignified science; and with its present im-
petus and its future certainty of development, it is
destined to startle the world by its marvelous revelations.

### HISTORY OF HYPNOTISM.

The germ of the science of hypnotism was recognized by the ancient Greeks and Romans, who derived their knowledge of it from the early Egyptians.
There is also evidence that the Chinese practiced the
art thousands of years ago. In fact, the exercise of
hypnotic power seems to have been one of the intuitive accomplishments of mankind; for in various

forms it is practiced by the untutored savage in all parts of the world. We may even go further and declare hypnotic power to be an attribute of all living creatures. Reptiles fascinate their victims; animals are all more or less awed by their superiors and in turn exercise power over their inferiors; male birds fascinate their mates, and even fishes are known to excite fear in their kind.

Bereft of its traditions, the history of hypnotism commences with the discoveries and experiments of Dr. Friedrich Anton Mesmer, who was born near Constance, Switzerland, May 23rd, 1734. He received his medical degree from the University of Vienna, and in his graduating thesis he introduced his theory of animal magnetism. This theory was that throughout the universe there was a power similar to the magnetic power of "loadstone," that exercised a peculiar influence over the human body. To this power he gave the name of "animal magnetism," and declared it could be excited by the personal contact of human beings under certain circumstances. He first published an account of his discoveries in 1775, enshrouding them in secrecy concerning his methods. The publication created great excitement and when he shortly afterward went to Paris, in 1778, genero s donations of money were given him by his admirers and those interested in his theories. The gov rnment made him a proposition to give him an a nuity of $4,000 a year and provide him a fully equ pped hospital free of expense

if he would impart his secret method to three persons
to be named by the authorities.  He refused to accept
the proposition, and continued to practice his art for
the cure of disease with great success and to teach
his methods to large numbers of pupils.  In this way
he derived a large income for several years, when in
1785 the government appointed a commission, including Bailly, Lavoisier and Benjamin Franklin, to
investigate his methods.  This committee made a
very unfavorable report, which destroyed Mesmer's
popularity and caused him to lose his practice and
pupils.  He returned to Switzerland, where he died
March 5th, 1815.

### THE MARQUIS ARMOND DE PUYSEGUR.

One of Mesmer's most enthusiastic scholars was
the French Marquis Armond De Puysegur.  He
greatly improved upon Mesmer's methods and discovered the manner of producing the somnambulistic
state, in which he was enabled to cure various
diseases without causing the violent hysterical
demonstrations that frequently followed Mesmer's
performances.  His discoveries, however, as well as
those of Mesmer, were apparently forgotten until
Du Patel and De Foissac, Parisian physicians, applied
them in their practice (1820-1830).

### BAIRD AND CURTIS.

The scientific career of hypnotism started in 1841,
under the impulse given it by Dr. James Baird, of
Manchester, England, who met with such great

success with it in his practice that other physicians and investigators followed his example. It was Dr. Baird who gave to the science the name of HYPNOTISM.

In America, the first physician of prominence to investigate and employ hypnotic power as an aid in the treatment of disease was Dr. Alva Curtis, whose book on "Medical Science," published in 1846, contains a section on "Neurology and Animal Magnetism," which gives full and explicit directions for using this power in medical practice. The position he then assigned to it was that of one of the harmless methods of aiding natural efforts toward restoring health. He bereft it of all sensationalism and treated it in a purely scientific manner.

## CHARCOT AND BERNHEIM.

In the '70's, Dr. Charcot, of Paris, became an enthusiastic hypnotist, and employed hypnotic suggestions with great success in the treatment of large numbers of patients in his hospital at La Salpetriere. His prominence as a physician led many others to follow his example. About the same time, Dr. H. Bernheim, Professor in the Faculty of Medicine, in Nancy, commenced his arduous investigations and experiments that have rendered his name famous in the field of hypnotic science.

In later years, many physicians and scientists of renown have added their labors to those of the investigators mentioned, and at the present time the

science has become so universally recognized that
departments of "suggestive therapeutics" are established in the leading medical colleges; and what was
formerly regarded as one of the tricks of charlatans
is now established as a useful and dignified science.

## DEFINITIONS.

HYPNOTISM is the science and art of mentally
controlling the thoughts and actions of others. Its
study embraces a knowledge of the methods best
adapted for developing personal mental power and
directing the mental activity of others.

The word HYPNOTISM, derived from the Greek
word hypnos, meaning sleep, has long been
accepted as the term under which all the varied
phenomena of the science are included. In reality
the word hypnotism is a misnomer, for it is not necessary for a person to be forced into hypnosis, or the
sleep-like state, before he can be mentally influenced.
But as this sleep-like state is readily induced and
often most desirable while producing the various
phenomena of mental control, it is more convenient
to class all these allied phenomena under the one
term than it would be to technically differentiate
them. The word hypnotism, then, will be used in its
broad sense throughout this volume, and the word
hypnosis will be employed to designate the special
sleep-like state which may be induced.

To HYPNOTIZE a person literally means to place
him in the sleep-like state; but as this state is not

absolutely necessary for mental control, the word hypnotize is now generally used to designate the act of mentally controlling the thoughts and actions of others, whether through the production of hypnosis or otherwise. Thus a speaker may hypnotize his audience or a business man may hypnotize his customers.

POST-HYPNOTISM or POST-SUGGESTION means the suggestion to a hypnotized person of some action which he will perform at some designated time after he has been awakened.

AUTO-SUGGESTION is the suggestion which a hypnotized person gives himself; for instance, when angered by an imaginary wrong, resentment will usually be an auto-suggestion. The term is also used to designate suggestions which persons make to themselves when inducing self-hypnosis. An ordinary example of this is the setting of a special time to awaken, just before going asleep.

THE OPERATOR is the person who hypnotizes another by the production of actual hypnosis.

THE SUBJECT is the person who is hypnotized or to whom hypnotic suggestions are effectively made.

MESMERISM is one form of hypnotism, but the term is now employed to designate the method of producing the sleep-like condition by means of passes. It is so called in honor of Dr. Fr. Anton Mesmer. Animal magnetism, magnetic influence and hypnotic influence are various terms employed in expressing the power used in gaining mental control over others.

A SITTING is the voluntary private submission of any person to the hypnotic influence of another.

A SEANCE is the performance of hypnotic experiments in the presence of a few selected persons.

AN EXHIBITION is the public demonstration of the various degrees of hypnotism, given for amusement or scientific purposes.

# CHAPTER I.

## PHILOSOPHY OF HYPNOTISM.

Practical understanding of the subject—Hypnotism one of the
exact sciences—Relationship to other sciences—Analysis
of hypnotic phenomena—Practical illustrations—Explanation of hypnotic influence—Overcoming mental resistance—Mental action explained—Relationship of thought
to physical action—Involuntary actions—Day dream—A
well balanced mind—Relationships of operator and subject—Concentration of thought—Passive condition of the
mind—Transfer of thought to the seat of physical action—
Hypnotic performances are natural actions—First essentials—Hypnotism illustrated by object lessons—Hypnotic susceptibility not a sign of mental weakness.

It is not within the scope of this volume to enter
into a discussion regarding the relationship of "soul
and body," or to try to define in a technical manner
the changes that take place in brain cells during the
action of thought and the performance of voluntary
and involuntary physical actions. Such studies may
be interesting, but are suitable for other places in
literature.

It is the practical understanding of hypnotism that
is now most desirable. Sufficient data have been col-
lected and abundant investigations have been made
to permit numerous facts to be systematically arranged into what is termed the "Science of Hypno-

tism." This science has phenomena peculiar to itself, controlled by laws that belong neither to physiology, chemistry, physics or magnetism. They are the exclusive laws of hypnotism. By their observance we know absolutely that we can produce certain effects and that those effects are invariable,— that is, under similar conditions, similar results will always be obtained. This is as certain as the fact that when a chemical compound has been once formed, it is established forever that the same compound may be again formed whenever the identical .substances are placed under the same conditions.

We cannot produce chemical compounds by mere mechanical processes; for only chemical laws govern chemical phenomena. And so it is with every other branch of science; they are studies of themselves, no matter how intimately they may be associated. Hypnotism may seem to be closely connected with physiology or with magnetism or with electrical manifestations; but that seeming connection does not place its phenomena under control of the laws of any of those sciences.

### ANALYSIS OF HYPNOTISM.

The initial point of our knowledge of hypnotism is the fact that we can practically observe that it is possible for one person to mentally control the thoughts and actions of another person; and that the person controlled cannot ordinarily regain his individual power to think and act for himself until permitted to do so by the person controlling him.

It is well to analyze this fact and satisfactorily explain it to ourselves, that we may have a basis upon which to build our knowledge of hypnotic phenomena. By way of illustration let us consider one of the simplest examples.

A hypnotist has seated before him a subject with whom he intends to experiment. Apparently there is little difference between them; both seem sound in mind and body; still one assumes at once to direct the other, who obeys. This may be by agreement; but evidently no lot was cast as to who should command and who should obey. It seems to have been decided by mutual consent, or rather not to have been decided at all, but simply to have been taken for granted. One assumes the role of operator and consequently the other becomes at once the subject. The one asserts a superiority and the other instantly manifests a greater or less degree of submission. No words to this effect have been spoken and no physical force has been employed to produce it, nevertheless it is realized by all parties interested.

The operator directs the subject to assume certain positions, which are assumed at once. He says but few words; but every request made is instantly obeyed. The subject is able to voluntarily withdraw his attention and refuse obedience, but chooses to, or rather simply does, remain and follow whatever instruction is given him.

The operator makes certain movements and then

utters assertions which are heard and believed by the subject, who manifestly has relinquished all independence. He believes the most absurd statements and at a mere suggestion from the operator performs all manner of actions and zealously applies himself to any task assigned him, real or imaginary. In fact, whatever the operator wills and suggests that the subject performs.

Such is an example of ordinary hypnotism, where the operator has mentally influenced the thoughts and actions of the subject; and we must establish in our own minds a satisfactory explanation of how the influence was obtained and obedience enforced. The subject's transition from voluntary submission to involuntary obedience was apparently gradual; yet there must have been an instant when the change was made.

We can, by way of illustration, compare this performance to the gradual addition of weights to one side of a pair of scales to counteract the pressure exerted by some heavy substance on the other side. Little by little additional weights are added until the balancing point is reached and then passed. Similarly, the will of the operator gradually overcomes the resistance of the subject and when the balancing point has been passed there is no more resistance and the subject is hypnotized.

To carry the illustration further, when the profound stage of hypnotic sleep has been produced, the operator's will may be compared to one side of the scale completely loaded down with weights; while the subject's will is nothing in comparison. It makes no impression, whatever, and does not enter into the question of balance.

In testing a new subject it is always uncertain just how much will power may be necessary to cause submission; and the act of hypnotizing is usually gradual. When a subject has been thoroughly controlled, it is comparatively easy to again hypnotize him; or, carrying out the illustration, knowing the pressure upon one side of the scale, the weights to counterbalance it may be applied at once.

Experience soon demonstrates to an operator the degree of effort he must exert to hypnotize a subject; and the most expert hypnotist occasionally meets with persons whom he quickly perceives to be beyond his powers of influence.

### BASIS OF HYPNOTIC INFLUENCE.

In order to intelligently perform any action it is necessary to have an understanding of what it is proposed to do. The act of hypnotizing others is entirely a mental process; but just what that process is very few really comprehend. There is an ill-defined idea of what mental action means, but usually that idea is more confusing than lucidating.

To the practical hypnotist it matters little what theories of mental philosophy are most generally accepted. He is more concerned in fixing in his own mind a basis of action and of placing his ideas

in such a shape as will best enable him to comprehend the character of his work. This much can be
clearly realized: Thought always precedes voluntary
action; but there may be action without any apparent thought and thought without any apparent
action. For examples:

1. A man sees an arbor well laden with grapes,
the sight suggests a desire to enjoy the fruit and that
desire suggests the intention to procure some of it,
thus far there has been only thoughts in connection
with the grapes and these thoughts then suggest
the action of walking over to the arbor and picking
them and eating them, which constitutes a voluntary
act preceded by thought. In other words, the mental thought was conveyed to the seat of physical action and the result followed.

2. A child touches its finger to the hot stove and
immediately withdraws it. Here is action without
any apparent thought directing it; for the child's
mind was passive and did not contemplate that when
the hot stove was touched, the finger would suffer
and should therefore be withdrawn. The withdrawal
of it was involuntary, for he could not have continued to hold it against the stove if he had so desired. The impression made upon the brain was one
of pain, which automatically suggested the physical
withdrawal of the finger. This is an illustration of
physical action without any apparent thought. Such
instances occur to everyone daily. Blinking the
eyes when there is danger to them, shrinking or

jumping to one side when there is an explosion near
by; keeping our bodies from rolling out of bed when
we are asleep, are all familiar examples of what we
call involuntary actions. They are suggested to the
brain and the suggestion is carried out instantly
without time being taken for actual thought.

3. Examples of thought without any apparent action are familiar to everyone. Such occur constantly
in every mind. Mentally we can see ourselves acting various parts in life; and in our "day dreams"
we become heroes or men of note, or Napoleons of
finance. But, alas! for the most part the thoughts
we entertain remain where they are conceived. They
too often fail to be conveyed to the seat of physical
action. We have within ourselves the power to restrain our thoughts and prevent ourselves from "carrying them out." When we do not possess that
power, then we become maniacs, unable to control
our physical actions, which are aroused by our
thoughts.

The well balanced mind, then, may be likened to
a most ingeniously contrived machine. Impressions
from without produce effect upon the department
of thought and this effect may be, at our pleasure,
conveyed to or prevented from entering the department of physical action. At times the department
of thought may be idle and impressions quickly pass
from it to the seat of physical actions, then spoken
of as involuntary.

In the study and practice of hypnotism it will be

found useful to bear in mind the above illustrative examples as aids in comprehending what takes place during a hypnotic sitting. The subject, take it for granted, is a sane and healthy person capable of thinking for himself and of voluntarily acting upon what has been suggested by his thoughts. He is also capable of restraining his impulses to act; and, like others, his physical actions are frequently performed involuntarily, being prompted by impressions suddenly made upon his mind and instantly conveyed to the seat of physical action without being dwelt upon as thoughts.

The operator calls attention to some one object or sound or motion, with the idea of concentrating the subject's thought entirely upon it. The subject voluntarily allows his attention to be concentrated and before long the monotony of the concentration of thought makes it difficult for him to voluntarily conceive any other thoughts and consequently his mind becomes what is known as passive—a blank regarding other matters.

While the subject's mind is in this passive condition, the operator quickly and sharply utters a suggestion. It is so suddenly impressed upon his mind that without reflection it is at once conveyed to the seat of physical action and almost involuntarily the suggestion is carried out, just as the child quickly withdraws his finger from the hot stove before he has learned to think of what is necessary to do under the circumstances.

Again, as in Example 3, the subject may be induced to so completely concentrate his thoughts and refrain from all manifestations of physical action, that it will be possible for the operator to suddenly impress upon him that even all thought must cease entirely, and the profound hypnotic condition will follow.

In all hypnotic performances the subject is simply acting the part of a sane and healthy person, and exhibiting his natural capabilities. No injury has been done to him. He has concentrated his thought under influences exerted by the operator and his mind becomes passive under these same influences, just as it might be possible for it to become under certain circumstances if no operator were present. The suggestions made by the operator are received and conveyed to the seat of physical action just as sensations of pain or joy or grief are frequently impressed upon the mind and followed by appropriate demonstrations before any plan of what manifestations should be made could be planned or even thought of. It is to such conditions we refer when we say, for instance: "He involuntarily cried out," "he jumped for joy," "he writhed in agony," etc. The suggestion was made suddenly upon the mind when not expected and the result followed naturally.

Similarly the operator's suggestions are made and the subject's actions naturally follow. Let it always be borne in mind, then, that in order to "hypnotize" skill must be exerted to render the subject's mind as passive as possible. This is the first essential and cannot be disregarded. Next, it is necessary to utter introductory suggestions sharply and decisively as commands that necessitate immediate obedience. When the instant transfer of suggestions to the seat of physical action has been established, then, and then only, can suggestions be made in a less emphatic manner.

### PRACTICAL ILLUSTRATION.

Another practical method of illustrating hypnotic control may be of great service to beginners in forming a figurative idea of what must be accomplished and how it must be accomplished. Object lessons may seem simple methods of teaching; but their simplicity always renders them effective when properly applied.

In the following diagram, let A and B represent two telegraph operators, seated side by side, sending various and different messages to the ends of their respective lines, represented by X and Y. A conceives the idea that

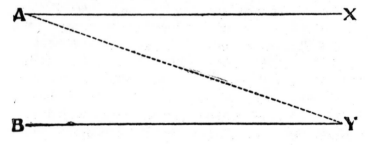

he would like to transmit his own messages to Y over B's line, and calls B's attention to some special object of interest and succeeds in so completely attracting his attention that he is enabled to connect his own line with B's, as shown by the dotted lines. A can therefore transmit whatever messages he may desire and instead of their being received at the end of his own line, X, they will be received at Y, the end of B's line.

Again, without trying to detract B's attention, he may propose the connection of his line, and be absolutely refused the privilege, and then set to work to make the connection by force, and if stronger than B he may overpower him and transmit his messages as desired.

Or, after expressing his wish to B to send messages over his line, B may readily give his consent and cease to use his own instrument and allow it to lie idle while the connection is being made, and the result accomplished will be satisfactory.

The practical application of these illustrations may serve a most excellent purpose to beginners in hypnotism. Let A and B represent the thought centers of two individuals and X and Y their respective centers of physical action. That is, when A conceives a thought he can at his pleasure transmit it to his own center of physical action and carry out his desires by physical manifestations. For instance, let him conceive the thought of walking and voluntarily he wills to walk, his thought has been sent to X, and immediately his legs begin to move and he walks. B, near him, is also entertaining thoughts and carrying out his conceptions in a similar manner.

A wishes to hypnotize B. That is, he desires to compel B to do whatever he may suggest. To accomplish this he manages to concentrate B's thoughts upon some object or occurrence and while the mind is thus comparatively passive he suddenly "makes connection" with B's mind and his suggestions are immediately transmitted to B's center of physical action and carried out by B in an involuntary manner.

The request to hypnotize him may not be well received by B, but through fear or inferior will power he may be forced to yield, and the result will be precisely the same.

Again, B may desire to be hypnotized and enter heartily into the arrangement and be able to facilitate matters greatly by his aid. As a rule, subjects who have been hypnotized a few times throw aside all doubt and fear and greatly help the operator.

Many persons believe that only the weak-minded can be readily hypnotized. This is not so, for they often prove to be difficult subjects. On the other hand, a very highly intelligent person who has his mind and thoughts completely under control, and who can render himself completely passive, may be hypnotized with the greatest ease, if he is interested in the subject of hypnotism and yields himself to the operator's influence. Otherwise intellectual capacity does not enter much into hypnotic susceptibility, which is controlled by other factors.

Occasionally, during an attempt to hypnotize a new subject, the operator may find himself utterly unable to accomplish his purpose, and the concentration of his own thought upon the single idea of producing hypnosis being continued without effect for some time may render him passive toward his subject, and thus reverse the relationship of the parties. The would-be operator then becomes the subject, and is himself hypnotized. Such an occurrence is rare; but its possibility serves as a warning to operators who persist in repeated fruitless efforts to hypnotize others who are capable of exercising great will power in their resistance.

# CHAPTER II.

## QUALIFICATIONS OF A HYPNOTIST.

Natural talent and special adaptability—Hypnotic power unknowingly possessed by many—Bodily health and strength —A sound mind in a sound body—Self-confidence—Determination to succeed—Exercise of will power—Fearlessness—Concentration of thought—Quick perceptive powers—Self-possession.

All healthy persons possessing intelligence and self-confidence can, by practice, exercise hypnotic power over others to a greater or less degree, according to their natural ability. Still, comparatively few become expert hypnotists. In this art, as in all others, special adaptability is a prominent requisite to success. For instance, anyone can learn to play the piano and by practice may become mechanically and technically proficient in music; but only a few are true musicians with souls filled with harmony. The same may be said of the art of painting, which is taught everywhere, but in which the most arduous study and practice cannot give the soul-inspiring results which follow the touch of the true artist's brush.

The world ever remembers such geniuses as Mozart, Beethoven, Liszt, Wagner, Michael Angelo, Rembrant, Raphael, Sir Joshua Reynolds, West,

Rosa Bonheur and others of similar natures. That all cannot become like them is no reason why others should not try to beautify the world by art and make it more joyful by music, rendered to the best of their abilities.

Hypnotism, taking its rank with the other arts and sciences, should be similarly considered. It has its men of note, who have mastered its mysteries and accomplished wonders by its powers. Most of them were endowed by nature with special hypnotic ability. Others are equally well endowed who are not yet conscious of the fact. All may succeed in learning it to the best of their abilities and through it accomplish much good for themselves and those about them.

The successful hypnotist should possess GOOD HEALTH. Bodily ailments usually diminish mental power and always lower vitality. A strong and vigorous physique exerts a great influence upon those of less favored bodily condition. Still, mere physical development does not signify that a person is a good hypnotist; for the mental characteristics must be equally developed. A sound mind in a sound body constitutes the basis of hypnotic ability.

SELF CONFIDENCE is the hypnotist's most necessary qualification; without it he can accomplish nothing. If he possess no faith in his own power, he cannot induce others to yield to him. In practicing the art of hypnotism let him above all things cultivate self-confidence. But let that self-confidence be backed by manifest ability. One must actually possess power before he is able to exercise it.

DETERMINATION to succeed in whatever is undertaken will greatly aid the student of hypnotism. Many failures may possibly be experienced at the start, but they should be only incentives to try again. Let the failures and their surroundings be carefully analyzed and let the causes be ascertained and avoided in the next experiments. Success must follow when all precautions are observed and the necessary manipulations and mental influences employed. As a rule, those who make their first attempts to hypnotize others become embarrassed and discouraged, for the reason that they are too ready to "give up." It is practice that is required in this art as in every other, and unless an operator is naturally endowed with marvelous hypnotic powers he can reach perfection only through practice.

WILL POWER is a most fortunate possession for the hypnotist, and if he does not possess it by nature he should cultivate it. Some persons easily control others merely by the force of their will. They make excellent hypnotists. It is this power which raises a volunteer from the ranks to the generalship of an army. He is born to command. We notice such persons in all walks of life, under all conditions and at all ages. Even among boys at play there will be some one who will control the others by his will power, and his fellows will obey him without hesitation. There is also the same trait through the whole world of living creatures. By seemingly common consent flocks of birds follow their leaders and herds of animals follow their leaders.

To persons capable of exerting this will power, hypnotizing others will be a comparatively easy task. To those who cannot easily exert it, the practice of the art may at first be difficult. But will power, like every other mental attribute, is developed by exercise, and may be acquired by even those most lacking it in their natures.

FEARLESSNESS or the willingness to dare without hesitation, will be found most serviceable to the hypnotist. If he should be afraid to experiment upon his subject, or afraid he cannot awaken or control those whom he hypnotizes, he should never undertake such work.

Fear unnerves anyone, and persons willing to submit themselves to the operator, to be placed under his power, are quick to discern the least manifestation of timidity, and that is fatal to the successful production of hypnosis. The operator must at all times make the subject realize—not by words, but by manner—that he is absolutely devoid of fear.

CONCENTRATION OF THOUGHT.—It is always absolutely necessary for the hypnotist to be able to fix his mind wholly upon one train of thought. Many fail in their first attempts, because they allow a multitude of thoughts to flit through the mind while conducting experiments. For instance, they are all the time wondering if they actually will succeed, and think what effect their success will have on others, and imagining what possibilities the future might bring to them if they should succeed. It is surprising what a multitude of varied thoughts the mind is capable of entertaining, seemingly at one time, and still be striving to perform some special work.

Here, again, practice is valuable. The student of hypnotism should, by all means, learn to concentrate his thoughts, for in his work, as in every other line of work, an ability to do so is invaluable. To keep the mind on one thing may not be an easy task at first, but it must be accomplished before success can be attained.

PERCEPTION.—Quick perceptive powers will enable a hypnotist to instantly realize the peculiar characteristics of his subjects and to notice the effect his efforts are having upon them. All subjects cannot be hypnotized by the same methods. Some yield readily to mysterious words and movements; others are impressed best by music or monotonous sounds; others require passes or manipulations; and, again, in some cases, fear of the operator must be aroused, while in others their complete confidence must be obtained.

The study of human nature becomes very important in connection with hypnotism, and the habit of quickly observing minute details should be cultivated. In choosing subjects it is valuable and in controlling them while under hypnotic influence it may save much trouble and annoyance.

SELF-POSSESSION is always very desirable. A person who "loses his head" will make a poor hypnotist. Occasions are constantly arising where the self-possession of the operator is of the utmost importance. For example, a subject may not awaken at once when commanded to do so, which will require either some other suggestion quickly made or the adoption of another method of awakening. If there should be the least hesitation or loss of self-control, those witnessing the performance would be quickly thrown into a state of consternation. Again, it frequently happens that a new subject will not readily yield and will manifest the most stubborn resistance to all efforts to hypnotize him. The operator must not then lose his self-possession and pronounce the attempt a failure or abandon it without suitable comment, such as, "Well, that was pretty well done; you're a difficult subject; but you can be hypnotized;" or, "I will hypnotize you when the conditions are more favorable; there is something disturbing you and we'll have to find out what it is." Never should the least discomfiture be manifested. It detracts from the operator's power and self-confidence; it weakens the susceptibility of his subjects and causes spectators to lose confidence in his ability.

# CHAPTER III.

## QUALIFICATIONS OF A SUBJECT.

Percentage of persons capable of being hypnotized—Natural antagonisms—Discordant and harmonious vibrations— Who are good subjects—Feeble-minded not always easily hypnotized—Strong-minded persons may make excellent subjects—Concentration of thought—Laboring men—Following a leader—Mobs easily led by suggestion—Murat Halsted and the strikers—Farmers not easily hypnotized at home—The confidence man—Slaves and servants—Climate has an influence—Susceptibility of men and women —Precautions necessary in hypnotizing women—Hysterical attacks—Emotional persons—Nationality—Dutch— Scandinavians—East Indians—French—Italians — Americans—Influence of age.

An expert hypnotist should be able to hypnotize ninety out of every hundred persons he may attempt to influence. Some of these will be affected much more readily than others, and with a few he will have great difficulty. The ten that he is unable to hypnotize may easily fall under the influence of other hypnotists.

It is a fact which we realize in our everyday life that there exist natural antagonisms between certain persons without any apparent cause. Very often we hear the remark: "I can't bear to be near her; she makes me feel creepy, and I don't know why." Some people declare such natural antagonisms are due to "discordant vibrations," and that the immediate friendships that sometimes spring up "on first sight," are due to "harmonious vibrations." These pronounced likes and dislikes may be explained according to various theories; but the fact remains that they exist and they play an important part in the relationships of human beings. A person cannot readily hypnotize anyone who experiences personal antagonism; and he can, as a rule, easily gain control over those who "take a liking" to him.

### WHO ARE GOOD SUBJECTS?

It has often been asked, "What kind of persons are most readily hypnotized?" Some imagine that blondes succumb easiest to hypnosis and others have their reasons for thinking that brunettes make the best subject. But the question of light and dark or ruddy or pale complexion does not exert any influence.

As a rule, it is commonly believed that feeble minded persons are most easily influenced, and a great many think that anyone who has been hypnotized must necessarily lack strength of character. "Oh, no, you can't hypnotize me. I'm too strong-minded," is a remark often heard by the hypnotist. But let such persons beware how they accept a dare from the hypnotist. They may, under most circumstances, be able to "resist," but when all surroundings are right, they will yield as readily as others.

It is untrue that a good subject is always weak-minded and has no self-control. The fact is, a person who has absolute control over his own mind, and is able to render himself perfectly passive and enter into the full spirit of the phenomenon of hypnotism, always makes the best subject. But such a person cannot easily be persuaded to allow himself to be hypnotized. He usually wishes to perform the work of hypnotizing others.

When we consider the philosophy of hypnotism, and that it involves the principle of mental impressions being made upon a passive mind by causing that mind to concentrate all thought upon a single idea, we get at the key to choosing good subjects.

The modern factory hand, filling a subordinate position, has been accustomed to implicitly obeying the commands of his "boss." He has learned to concentrate his thoughts upon one idea, and to drive all other ideas from his mind while at work. He has learned these things through fear of "losing his job" and through the constant "driving" of the boss to get as much work from him as possible. Manifestly he makes a good hypnotic subject, and with no discredit to himself. It is his habit of life that renders him such.

Notice how quickly an army of laboring men can be swayed by the impressive statements of a leader, and influenced to perform acts that their cool judgment on reflection would not countenance. Jail deliveries, lynchings and the like, are examples of such influence. It is no indication of a lack of intelligence, but simply a natural result of training. Mobs look for a leader whom they may follow. The majority of those composing mobs are employes accustomed to obey; their rash acts are manifestations of hypnotic influence. With equal ease they could be influenced to desist from demonstrations of all kinds. Let a man of influence, accustomed to command and to have his commands obeyed, step forth and resolutely order quiet and a return to reason, and the tumult will subside.

A number of years ago, when the famous and venerable editor, Murat Halstead, was proprietor of the Cincinnati Commercial, a strike of considerable proportions occurred among the printers of the city, who met, and in angry frame of mind, surrounded the Commercial office and made ugly demonstrations and violent threats. It was a tumultuous mob on the verge of creating ruin. Suddenly the imposing form of Murat Halstead appeared, standing upon a chair in the doorway of the office, facing the mob. They were ready to destroy his whole plant; but with a wave of the hand he attracted their attention and with a resolute look in his eyes and the utterance of the single word "silence," in a commanding voice, he instantly hushed the violent demonstrations; the crowd respectfully listened to his short explanations and assurances and upon his order to go quietly to their homes and reason over the matter awhile, the mob quietly dispersed. All he said and more had been read by every one present in the morning's paper over his signature, without effect. His presence, his actions and his voice and his mental power over minds accustomed to obey worked the change.

Farm laborers are not so readily placed under hypnotic control. The character of their work gives them more time to think and requires less concentration of thought. No one can guess what is passing through the mind of the boy on the farm as he drives the plow or performs his other work. He may be day dreaming or laying plans or scheming for the future. He is the boy who is apt to be heard of in after years as a great financier or general or statesman. There is a spirit of independence acquired on the farm that is denied the city factory hand. Farmers are not easily controlled by political bosses; they are usually independent voters. They are not easily hypnotized, because their habits of life have not limited their mental activities. Their tendency is to diffusion of thought and not to concentration. It is difficult to render their minds passive, but when the hypnotist places them under his control they become good subjects by practice.

It should be mentioned, that out of their natural environment the farmers are more readily hypnotized. For instance, in coming to a city, the unusual scenes and the multitude of sounds and objects to which they have not been accustomed, create confusion of thought in the mind which is then readily concentrated by hypnotic influence; such as the confidence man exerts upon his victim.

Persons accustomed to absolutely obey without question nearly always make good hypnotic subjects. Slaves are excellent examples of this fact. In our own country the African race are easily influenced; and this is especially true of those who were born in slavery. The wild scenes of "colored camp meetings" and revivals are one form of hypnotic demonstrations. Under the influence of religious fervor and the monotonous exhortation of the leader and the harmony of their musical songs they are swayed by the least suggestion, and in times of intense excitement about the altar many will contort their bodies or fall over benches without any apparent pain, or drop down in a state of catalepsy.

In India the native servants become good subjects on account of similar habits of obedience and the training of the mind to obey their master's commands.

### CLIMATE AND SEX.

Climate exerts a marked influence upon the susceptibility of subjects. Persons born and raised in the tropical regions are more easily hypnotized than those raised in cold climates; and in them it is usually an easy matter to induce profound hypnosis and the intense degrees of hypnotism.

Men usually make better subjects than women; although some men have a peculiar power over women, that is in reality a hypnotic control. Such men cannot usually control other men with any satisfaction.

In hypnotizing women, extra precautions must be taken to avoid unpleasant results. They are more emotional than men, and are liable to give way to their feelings in the midst of an exhibition. Instances are not infrequent where women have fainted while under the influence of hypnosis—some especially sad or harrowing sight having been suggested. Again, it is possible to throw women into hysterical conditions. They should never be suddenly awakened from hypnosis while in the midst of exciting suggestion, for they are extremely liable to "go into hysterics" and create a scene. Under such conditions, before awakening them, always make some pleasing suggestion, so that the mind will be calm upon awakening.

It may be mentioned here that women accustomed to spells of hysterics may be most appropriately treated through hypnotism. By mental influence a quietude of mind may be secured and by proper suggestions future attacks of hysterics may be averted.

Persons who are easily impressed by occurrences and rendered emotional by slight excitement, make good subjects. Their minds become accustomed to quickly concentrating their thoughts upon one idea to the exclusion of all others. Everything else is lost sight of while under the influence of some sudden joy or grief or unusual sight.

## NATIONALITY.

Nationality enters into hypnotic susceptibility. The French, Spaniards and Italians make good subjects, and the large majority of these people can be easily hypnotized.

The Dutch or inhabitants of Holland are, as a rule, difficult subjects. They are stoical and unemotional and resist attempts at coercion—priding themselves upon their independence and their ability to maintain their steadfastness of purpose.

The Scandinavian laboring classes are excellent subjects, although in most of them it takes considerable practice to be able to induce profound hypnosis with ease.

The inhabitants of the East Indies are by all means the most desirable of subjects; their habits of life and dispositions and climatic and social influences all beinc most conducive to their susceptibility to hypnotic control.

Americans, as a rule, make good subjects when they agree to be hypnotized and aid the operator, but they can seldom be forced into the hypnotic state against the will, as their independence of thought and action must be regarded as unfavorable influence. Still, American girls who are of a romantic turn of mind prove to be most excellent subjects.

Age affects the qualifications of a subject. Between fifteen and twenty-one years of age persons are usually most susceptible to hypnotic influence. Although young children often yield readily to general hypnosis, they cannot always be used as subjects for the profound stages, such as catalepsy and lethargy.    It is best not to experiment upon young children except under necessity, as parents and friends are apt to blame the operator for any subsequent sickness or peculiarities that might occur, which would in no way be a result of hypnotic influence.

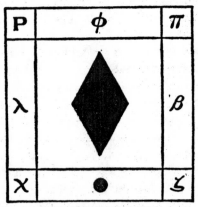

THE GRECIAN MIRROR.

# CHAPTER IV

## FAVORABLE AND UNFAVORABLE INFLUENCES.

Circumstances and surroundings—Hypnotizing stubborn subjects—Influence upon others—Avoidance of failures—New experiments—The experimenting room—Influence of light and darkness—Sunlight and colors—Temperature—Intense heat and drafts of air—Examples—Physical suffering—Agreeable and disagreeable odors—Perfumes—Tobacco smoke—Loud and discordant sounds—Music—Lullaby—Chants—Monotonous sounds—Melody—Music boxes—Singing of Angels—Soothing influence of music—Insanity and melancholy—Noise and quietude—Hypnotizing new subjects—Personal comfort—Position—The Chair—Clothing—Recumbent position—Emotions—Fear of being hypnotized—Fascination of Reptiles—Recognition of superior power—Domestic grief—Anger—Tranquillity of mind—Condition of the skin—Dryness—Influence of time.

Circumstances and surroundings have great influence in favoring or preventing hypnosis, and it is well to become thoroughly familiar with established facts in this connection. Not infrequently a good hypnotist finds it almost, if not altogether, impossible to control a subject whom he knows to be susceptible—the failure being due to improper circumstances or surroundings.

It is not always necessary to have the conditions perfect, for very frequently hypnosis is easily produced under the most unfavorable influences. But it is always easier upon the operator and more satisfactory to all parties concerned to take advantage of every favorable influence. To say the least, it is vexatious for an operator to have to battle with a subject. If he is a beginner, he loses confidence in himself, which is fatal to good results, and he exhausts his nervous energy.

To strive to hypnotize a stubborn subject, with determination that it must be done, strains the mental powers just as the physical powers are strained by exertions expanded in accomplishing results that require the full limit of muscular effort.

Another important reason for having circumstances as favorable as possible is the influences of success or failure upon others. There are always many skeptical persons anxious to exaggerate every seeming failure, and for an operator to manifest his inability to perform what he claims to be able to accomplish, is disastrous. Besides shaking the faith of others in his pretentions, it lowers his powers in the estimation of many whom he might desire to use as subjects, and sometimes shakes his confidence in himself. Nothing succeeds so well as success, is as true in hypnotism as it is in every other line of action.

To make a reputation as a hypnotist, it is necessary that there should be no failures in public. Do not undertake before others what you feel sure you cannot accomplish. Try new experiments privately. The following influences favorable and unfavorable to hypnotic control should be studied carefully. The favorable influences are not all necessary, but they are all conduccive to "making" good subjects, and a subject once well "made" can, with rare exceptions, be successfully exhibited in public, even under the most unfavorable circumstances.

## THE EXPERIMENTING ROOM.

In conducting experiments, especially with beginners, it is best to have a room isolated as much as possible from the rest of the house, so as to avoid interruptions and the distraction of the subject's mind by the noises of the household. For this reason also the room should be remote from the street, the walking of pedestrians and the movements of vehicles being liable to interrupt the perfectly passive state of mind which is requisite to successful hypnosis.

The furniture of the room should be plain and no unusual pictures or bric-a-brac should be displayed to attract attention. Carpet on the floor will prevent any noise from walking or from the movement of chairs. When there is no carpet, rubber buttons should be placed on the legs of chairs. It is very annoying to get a subject almost under control and then accidentally arouse him by the noise of a moving or creaking chair.

White, glaring walls are not good, neither are brilliant or grotesque hangings. Plain unfigured wall paper of a subdued tint will be found most favorable.

## INFLUENCE OF LIGHT.

A mild, subdued light aids the hypnotic influence, while a strong and bright light is a pronounced hindrance. Red and yellow are especially unfavorable colors and such globes or lamp shades should not be used, for they give a glare to everything in the room and tire the eyes. Such lights in a room make ordinary sleeping difficult and their effect in delaying the securement of hypnotic sleep will be found very noticeable.

A soft, blue light will aid the operator. It rests the eyes and consequently rests the brain, and more than any other light, it favors sleep. Do not use a dark blue shade, for that would attract attention by its peculiarity. If blue is not obtainable, a pale green may be used. Of course, the subject is not to look directly at the light; he is simply to realize the benefit of the diffused, soft tone cast about the room.

Bright sunlight should not be admitted. In the daytime a room with north windows is best, and cloudy days are more favorable than bright ones. When shades are used, blue or green are to be preferred. Always allow plenty of light in the room, so that the subject need not make an effort to look at objects to which you call his attention. But never admit a strong light.

## INFLUENCE OF TEMPERATURE.

A comfortable temperature, between 68 degrees and 78 degrees, will be found most favorable for inducing hypnosis; and, as a rule, the farther the departure from these limits the more difficult it becomes to gain control over a subject.

An expert hypnotist was invited by a body of scientific men to give a special exhibition of his powers, to illustrate his method of inducing hypnosis. He selected his best subject, and met the scientists by appointment in a suburban home, one intensely hot afternoon in July. But imagine his chagrin and the disappointment of the others, when he utterly failed to do more than render the subject drowsy. The intense heat, the short trip on the train and the unusual circumstances pertaining to the occasion, had all tended to disturb the subject's nervous equilibrium in such a manner that hypnosis could not be induced.

Such instances are rare in good subjects, but that they do occasionally occur illustrates the importance of observing all possible precautions and of taking advantage of such favorable influences as can be secured while trying to "break in" a new subject or while endeavoring to develop hypnotic power.

During a public exhibition, given by a celebrated hypnotist one cold winter night, the dozen or more subjects upon the stage all manifested pronounced signs of awakening in the midst of a most interesting performance, and the operator was obliged to make many passes over them in order to retain control. The cause of the partial awakening was a very cold draught of air blowing across the stage from a window opened by the janitor for the sake of ventilation. The operator, as soon as he realized the cause, ordered the window closed and impressively stated to his subjects, "Now, you are all warm and comfortable."

The above instance well serves to illustrate a peculiar feature of the hypnotic condition. Actual physical suffering or discomfort, such as may be caused by heat or cold, is readily, and often most acutely experienced by the hypnotized subject, unless the operator has specifically impressed upon him that he does not experience it. And, again, when the temperature is normal, the subject may be made to think that it is intensely cold or intensely hot, without control over him being lost. Suggestion can overcome the effect of the most intense suffering, and unless suggestion of ease is made, physical suffering may cause awakening from the hypnotic state.

It is especially necessary for an operator to remember these facts when subjects are under his control. Various circumstances may occur to cause unpleasant physical sensations, and these must be quickly realized and hypnotic suggestions made accordingly.

### INFLUENCE OF ODORS.

Unpleasant odors in a room may delay or entirely prevent the production of hypnosis. Tobacco smoke is especially antagonistic to those not accustomed to it, and even after such subjects have been hypnotized they are liable to awaken or become unmanageable, when someone near them commences to smoke. Under such circumstances, if the operator realizes the cause of the disturbance, he should make some such suggestion to the subject as, "Can you smell that delightful incense burning? It is a delightful odor." These words will be sufficient to at once overcome the physical discomfort caused by the smoke.

An operator, especially a beginner, must be continually on the alert to avoid anything and everything that might possibly interfere with his success. For instance, remember that people do not like to detect the odor of onions or garlic on the breath of others. Never eat such articles if you intend to hypnotize subjects. The disagreeable sensation caused by the odor may overcome your hypnotic influence or render it difficult to place them under control. While the sensation can be overcome by suggestion if the subjects is disturbed by it while under control, suggestion is of no avail before hypnosis is produced.

As disagreeable odors are detrimental to hypnotic control, so agreeable or pleasant odors are excellent auxiliaries in producing hypnosis. Strong, sweet odors are especially useful. Perfume sprinkled about the room will aid the operator, and the presence of fragrant blooming flowers will always be found useful. The heliotrope is one of the best plants in this connection, and a number of them in the operating room will give a heavy, sweet odor, profound enough to be agreeably oppressive, and in a measure tranquillize the tendency to nervous irritability so often experienced by persons subjecting themselves to hypnotic influences for the first time. Lilacs and tuberoses are equally as useful as the heliotrope. Many persons cannot at any time inhale the odors from these flowers without being soothed and rendered drowsy, especially when in an atmosphere of quietude or solemnity.

### INFLUENCE OF MUSIC.

If "music hath charms to soothe the savage breast" it also has the power to soothe the minds of all subjected to its influence. A few soft, melodious tones repeated over and over again, in lullaby fashion, will greatly aid the production of hypnosis. Such sounds have been employed for centuries by the so-called "charmers" of animals and reptiles, and their employment by the modern hypnotist is of recognized advantage in many cases.

Loud and boisterous music or discordant sounds have a disturbing influence and will usually interfere with the inexperienced operator's success. A case is reported where a young woman was undergoing a surgical operation while under hypnotic influence, when suddenly a band of musicians began to play in the street and she was quickly awakened. Upon such an occurrence the operator should have presence of mind enough to say: "Listen to the music, it is beautiful," or make some similiar statement. There are always premonitory signs of awakening, which give opportunity for action, and one of the important items in connection with hypnotism is to constantly watch the subject and recognize these signs and act promptly in the right manner to avoid untimely awakening. The signs of awakening are given elsewhere.

In hypnotizing young children, there is no aid so effective as lullaby music. This is naturally used by all mothers, savage and civilized, while rocking their babes to sleep.

The more monotonous the music, the more effective it will be, provided it is melodious and not discordant or harsh. It is the low, soft, simple melody, composed of a few notes, and repeated over and over again, that helps to induce hypnosis.

Expert hypnotists who desire to practice their art as a profession should provide themselves with every aid procurable, so as to enable themselves to hypnotize the largest number possible of the persons who present themselves. They should provide a proper room, as described, and become familiar with every known means of influence. A useful article for such a person is a music box of good manufacture. This can be set to some simple air, such as "Sweet Home," and placed in a chest or closet or muffled in some way, so that the sounds are extremely soft, like whisperings of music, repeated innumerable times. The soft notes of a flute, played by a third person in an adjoining room, is often advantageous, but the tones must be continued without interruption until complete hypnosis is produced. Otherwise the premature cessation of the sounds would be very liable to suddenly undo the partial influence obtained.

One of the most interesting sights connected with a hypnotic exhibition is to look upon a number of subjects to whom the operator has said some such words as these:

"Listen, there is beautiful music.    Angels are singing and playing upon their harps."

There comes over the subjects an ecstasy that cannot be produced in any other way.    Some will strike the most graceful attitudes of listening, and all will wear an expression of sweet content and rapture that will render the most homely face charming.    It well illustrates the soothing influence of music upon the human mind and the possibilities that may come from its employment.

The suggestion of music should always be made to subjects being treated for melancholy or insanity in any form.    It gives positive relief in every instance, and when often repeated, its benefits will prove permanent and sometimes effect a positive cure.

### INFLUENCE OF QUIETUDE.

It is useless for a beginner to try to hypnotize a new subject in the midst of noise.    Occasionally this can be done when the subject is very susceptible or when he sees before him a number of hypnotized persons and becomes convinced that he also must succumb.

Quietude is always to be desired, and a quietude

that is so profound "that you can hear a pin drop" is best. In fact, a deathly stillness is one of the greatest aids to hypnotism when there is no object to distract the mind. Not infrequently it has been found difficult, if not impossible, to hypnotize a subject because little noises cannot be subdued. The creaking of a door on its hinges, the creaking of shoes, whisperings, ticking of a clock and any one of many other trifling noises, may completely undo the result of much patient work.

An operator wishing to hypnotize a new subject for the amusement of a party should not attempt to do so unless he can take the subject apart by himself so as to secure absolute quiet, otherwise he may bring upon himself unmerited ridicule for his failure. Of course, the members of such a party are all anxious to "see how it is done," but it is impossible to keep them quiet enough to warrant any attempt to hypnotize a new subject in their presence. It is better to refuse positively to entertain them than to run the risk of personal discomfiture.

### INFLUENCE OF EASE AND COMFORT.

The subject should be placed in an easy chair—one that is cushioned is best. The feet should touch the floor with comfort and there should be no possible cause for any feelings of uneasiness. If the room is heated artificially he should not be near enough to the source of heat to feel its marked influence, neither should he be in a draught. The stove or open fireplace or lamp should not be seen by him, as these things distract attention.

Always have the clothing comfortably loose. It is not best for a subject to be placed in the hypnotic state with the collar or corset or any other article feeling tight. A good hypnotist may disregard such things without any bad results, but the safest plan is always the best plan.

The author once experienced considerable difficulty in getting under control a subject often previously hypnotized, and it was some time before the discovery was made that a tight pair of shoes were pinching the feet.

Sick persons, unable to sit in a chair without fatigue, may be hypnotized in the recumbent posture, but under ordinary circumstances the sitting position will be found best.

### INFLUENCE OF THE EMOTIONS.

Fear of the operator renders the subject more pliable. Persons who are not easily hypnotized will often readily yield when they see others in the hypnotic state. That is why it is comparatively easy for a hypnotist, during an exhibition, to successfully make subjects of those whom he has never met before. There are always persons in the audience who are greatly impressed by the performance and who are in constant dread lest the hypnotist shall excercise his influence over them, and when he calls for volunteers, they are usually the first to respond, not through any desire to be hypnotized, but through fear, which unnerves them and impels them to volunteer.

This kind of fear is the same as that which causes the victims of venomous reptiles to stand still and tremble, even when there is opportunity for escape, or which impels persons to rush into danger. Ordinarily it is spoken of as "fascination." Animals are often "fascinated" by the looks of serpents, when they realize that they are in the presence of a power which is superior to them and capable of destroying them.

Persons who have met with recent financial troubles or family bereavement are usually difficult to hypnotize. They are in the habit of brooding over their misfortunes and concentrating their minds upon themselves, and are constantly thinking of their experiences—not allowing rest to their minds at any time.

Anger is another disturbing influence to the hypnotist. It destroys the equilibrium of the mind, which is so necessary for success. Persons of an irritable disposition, as a rule, make poor subjects.

It should also be mentioned in this connection that the operator, himself, should cultivate an evenness of temper and not allow trifling matters to disturb him. He may meet with great disappointment in his attempts to hypnotize subjects while he is harboring thoughts of anger or hatred.

Tranquility of mind always exerts a favorable influence upon the production of hypnosis. The mind at peace with all mankind becomes most readily passive. Likewise the mental equilibrium of the operator has great influence upon the subject. The irritable mother finds it difficult to rock her babe to sleep, while the mother whose mind is at perfect ease experiences no difficulty. The "putting to sleep" of an infant is one form of inducing hypnosis.

## CONDITION OF THE BODY.

The operator as well as the subject should not be in a state of fatigue, if the best success is desired. It is true that deep hypnosis may be secured in a person who is completely "tired out"—exhaustion being really an aid in such cases. But deep hypnosis is not always desirable, and it is often very disappointing to realize that a subject shows no disposition to respond to any other suggestion than that of sleep.

For an operator to be physically tired is frequently disastrous. His subject soon realizes the fact and may fail to succumb to the most ardent efforts to hypnotize him. Worse than this, when the operator is fatigued and the subject full of energy and vigor, the operator may actually hypnotize himself while endeavoring to get his subject under control, and may by such an act forever lose control over the subject.

Pain may render hypnosis difficult by keeping the subject's mind constantly upon himself. But when pain has produced exhaustion, the sufferer usually yields without much difficulty. Fever is another unfavorable condition, although much good can be accomplished placing feverish patients under control. In the low grades of fever hypnosis is more readily induced.

The condition of the skin is important. A moderately warm and dry skin is best for both operator and subject. Should either be bathed in perspiration, the result is liable to be unsatisfactory. During an exhibition the operator should have in his pockets several handkerchiefs, and occasionally wipe his hands. Silk handkerchiefs are best. A cold, clammy skin may prevent all action. Some persons habitually have their hands in such a condition, and they make poor subjects. Cold feet are also detrimental.

## INFLUENCE OF TIME.

The time of day is not important, except as it concerns the condition of the body. Early morning finds an empty stomach, which is not good, and directly after meals finds the act of digestion at its height, which is not desirable. Late in the evening, the inclination to sleep may render hypnosis comparatively easy, but then it may be difficult to get a satisfactory response to any suggestions besides those of sleep. From an hour to two hours after meals is usually the most favorable time for operating upon a subject. This applies to both the subject and the operator. An expert hypnotist can successfully use a trained subject at any time of day.

# CHAPTER V.

## PRECAUTIONS TO BE OBSERVED.

Reputation and safety of the operator—Welfare of the subject—Dangers of hypnotism no greater than ordinary—Little evil and great good—Compared with dangers of other branches of science—Exaggerated reports of harm—Presence of a third party—Accident to the operator—Danger reduced to a minimum—Rarely used unlawfully—Avoidance of sudden shock—Causes of danger—Weakness of the heart—Catalepsy—Physical injury—Staring at the sun—Change from darkness to light—Fascination—Falls and other causes of injury—Contortions—Jumping—Violent exercise—Eating injurious articles—Suggestions of death—Post-hypnotic cautions—Suffocation—Hypnotizing the feeble-minded—Insanity and crime—Liability of exciting anger—Avoiding misunderstandings—Relief from suggestions.

Hypnotism must be practiced judiciously for the reputation and safety of the operator as well as for the welfare of the subject. The reckless employment of hypnotic influence is not without its danger, just as there is danger in the reckless employment of any other means. It is absurd to condemn the science of hypnotism simply because of the harmful influences and dangerous conditions made possible through its use. With just as much propriety could we condemn the use of fire for heating purposes because it might possibly destroy the house, or the use of bathing because the bather might drown in the water, or the eating of meat or fish on account of the danger of choking.

The harm resulting from hypnotism is infinitesimal compared with the good it has accomplished. In fact, no art ever practiced has so little evil to be responsible for, either through intent or accident. The history of the practice of medicine is strewn with the lives of thousands sacrificed through experimentation or ignorance. Chemical manipulations have wreaked destruction for ages and the acquisition of chemical knowledge has too frequently been prompted by a desire to use its mysteries for the perpetration of crime.

Occasionally we hear of hypnotism being used for evil purposes, but investigation of every such case reported would reveal the fact that nearly every one was a gross exaggeration or an entire fabrication promulgated for sensational effect. Very rarely there is a grain of truth in the reports and when there is such a desire for sensationalism in connection with hypnotism it is remarkable that more evil has not been laid at its door, especially as it would be difficult for the blunders of a hypnotist to be kept quiet.

### PRESENCE OF A THIRD PARTY.

It is always best for an operator to have an assistant present whenever practicing upon subjects, and for personal safety this is imperative where the operator is a man and the subject a young girl or woman. Occasionally most serious charges might be preferred by well meaning or designing persons, and these charges might be difficult to refute. The experiences of physicians and dentists while administering chloroform or other anaesthetics should be remembered. It would be considered a manifestation of very poor judgment on the part of a member of either of these professions should he administer an anaesthetic to a patient without the presence of a third party. The hypnotist should not fail to always observe similar precautions.

Some persons believe that one of the greatest dangers in hypnotism is the possibility that the operator may suddenly die or become insane while the subject is under his control. An experienced hypnotist himself became possessed with the idea of this possible danger, and would not at any time hypnotize a subject without the presence of his assistant, and when he had placed the subject completely under control he would say:

"Now, if anything happens to me, you must obey my assistant; or if he interrupts me and orders you to do otherwise than what I have commanded, you must obey him and not me."

Where an operator seriously entertains such fears as sudden death, spells of unconsciousness or of insanity, he might well observe such extraordinary precaution, although it would be far better for him to desist from the practice of hypnotism altogether.

But it must be remembered that even should accident or death happen to the operator, the subject would be sure to awaken in course of time, although the time might be very long should the operator have said: "Now, you will sleep very, very soundly and no one but myself can awaken you." When we consider all the circumstances the danger is reduced to the minimum and should not be considered a factor in any case.

The chances of hypnotists inducing hypnosis for immoral or unlawful purposes are extremely rare. If such thoughts should enter the mind of persons desiring to be hypnotized for curative or other reasons, let them employ an operator of known integrity and then insist upon the presence of a third party. It should also be remembered that few persons can be forced into hypnosis, for the first time, against their will, and that under the most favorable circumstances many persons cannot be hypnotized at all, while chloroform will cause insensibility in everyone to whom it is administered, and an excessive quantity of it means certain death.

## AVOID SUDDEN SHOCK.

In health, under most favorable circumstances, shock is injurious to the mind and body. The sudden announcement of the death of a relative or the loss of fortune has been known to cause death in persons afflicted with heart disease or liable to apoplexy or other dangerous condition. Great fright has often unbalanced the mind, and violent exertions may produce serious conditions.

Whatever may become a source of danger at any time may be made a source of danger by the hypnotist. It must not be supposed that because a person is "only hypnotized," he runs no risk of danger. The mind and body are not changed in any way and both are susceptible to injury, for there is no charm about hypnosis.

It may be interesting to spectators to make a subject laugh and express the greatest of joy and then suddenly change his emotions to those of great and violent grief. But it is dangerous to do this if the subject has a weak heart or if he is liable to apoplexy. To him the shock is just as real and impressive as it would be were the sudden change from joy to grief an actual occurrence of real life.

CATALEPSY should not be suddenly induced in a subject whose heart is weak. The shock of realizing that he cannot move his muscles might possibly prove disastrous. If it is at all desirable to produce catalepsy in such subjects, it is best to prepare the mind for it by such words as: "Soon you will realize that you cannot move a muscle of your body. The sensation will be a pleasant one and it will not harm you, for I will give you the power to move again in a short time."

### PHYSICAL INJURIES.

It is not true, as many claim, that the subject's

body can be made to resist the destruction of heat, cold, blows, injuries, etc., while under hypnotic influence. He can be rendered insensible to the impressions produced by these things, but he cannot be rendered proof against their actual effects. It is cruelty to command a subject to pick up a live coal. He may do it without suffering at the time, if the suggestion is given that it will not burn, but the coal will nevertheless burn his flesh.

A subject might be induced to stare with wide open eyes at the glaring sun and he might obey without manifesting any discomfort, but blindness would certainly result, for which the hypnotist would be responsible.

It is also inadvisable to change suddenly from darkness to brightness or from brightness to darkness without first warning the subject by such words as: "Now, it is going to get very light," etc.

During the act of fascination do not suddenly remove the object of fascination without stating that you are about to do so, the shock might otherwise injure him.

Injuries may be received during the hypnotic state, which may cause the death of the subject or cripple him for life. It is true that hypnotized persons and somnambulists can often walk in dangerous places without falling, because they do not realize their danger and consequently do not lose their presence of mind. But if such persons should walk upon frail supports, their hypnotized state would not keep the supports from breaking, neither would it lessen the danger of walking on slippery places.

It is a common practice for hypnotists during an exhibition to make the subjects jump and leap and contort their bodies. This is all well, provided that care is taken to watch each one carefully so as not to permit any action that might strain the muscles or cause rupture or any other injury. Moderation is always best. It may be remarked that "they know enough not to hurt themselves." This is not true, for their whole mind is occupied in carrying out the suggestion, and does not take the least concern for personal safety. Violent excercise loses none of its injurious effects upon a hypnotized person.

Some of the most interesting experiments may be made by suggesting that harsh articles, such as nails, stones, etc., are articles of food, and directing that they should be eaten. This is always an indiscretion and liable to cause trouble. The suggestion of eating implies swallowing, and to swallow such articles means danger. Care must be taken, also, not to allow the mouth to be filled with powders, paper, or other substances that might cause strangulation when swallowed or inhaled. Such accidents are rare, because hypnotists are usually cautious about these things. Attention is here called to them for the purpose of making assurance doubly sure.

It is well known that while under the hypnotic influence, subjects can eat most obnoxious articles without realizing their unpleasant effects, provided

the proper suggestions are made.  It is possible to
give a subject a glass of diluted ammonia and say:
"Here, drink this glass of milk," and thus get him
to drink it.  But such an act would be grossly wrong,
for the ammonia would injure the throat and stomach, even though it were not strong enough to cause
strangulation and even though he experienced under
suggestion, a pleasurable sensation while swallowing it.

### SUGGESTIONS ABOUT DYING.

It is a well known fact that an operator can often
control the pulse rate of his subject by some such
suggestion as the following:

"Your pulse is beating very slowly.  Feel it and
notice how slow it is.  Why, it is down to fifty; now
it is forty, now it is thirty," etc.

This suggestion may be carried too far, even to
the point of causing the heart to cease beating altogether, which would mean death.  But this would be
difficult to accomplish in most instances.  Still it is
well to bear in mind the possibility of such a suggestion.

Another improper suggestion to make, would be,
"don't fall, or don't do so and so, for it will kill you."
This might act as a post-hypnotic suggestion and
prove disastrous should the subject ever meet with
the accident mentioned.  When a suggestion of
inability is made, it should always be followed with a
release, such as, "Now you can do it."  This will often

prevent unpleasant results, for hypnotic suggestions are capable of producing lasting impressions.

Similar precautions must be observed in suggesting irregularity of breathing. It is dangerous to suggest that the subject is suffocating and can't breathe. To do so may cause actual suffocation by allowing insufficient quantities of air to enter the lungs.

### HYPNOTIZING THE FEEBLE-MINDED.

It is a common belief that feeble-minded persons make the best subjects. This is not true, but nevertheless persons of weak mind may perhaps be readily induced to submit to hypnosis, and an inexperienced operator may avail himself of this opportunity to secure a subject. But this is unwise. The parents or friends of the feeble-minded person may not realize his mental incapacity until after he has been hypnotized, and then they are very liable to attribute his mental infirmity to the effect of hypnotism. Or it may be that everyone may realize that the subject is feeble-minded, and the operator's influence over him will be attributed entirely to that cause, which will not add anything to his reputation as a hypnotist. It is best, under all circumstances, to leave feeble-minded persons alone when looking for hypnotic subjects.

### SUGGESTIONS OF INSANITY AND CRIME.

It must be admitted that the mind may be injured by making positive hypnotic suggestions of insanity. It is unwise, to say the least, to cause a subject to consider himself insane. Such an impression, if long continued, might make a deep impression upon the mind and result disastrously unless relieved by a counter-suggestion, such as: "Now, you are perfectly sane again, your mind is all right."

To frequently suggest to a subject that he is a maniac, and allow him to persist in acting in accordance with such a suggestion, may render him extremely liable to become easily angered or mentally disturbed.

It is well to be careful in suggesting to a subject on exhibition that he is a thief or a drunkard and allow him to act the part. Of course, the suggestion will not make him either in his everyday life, but if he should become such, his friends and relatives would probably blame the operator. In a small community this would be very unpleasant, although most uncalled for and unjust. Relief from the suggestion always destroys the possibility of after effects, but this fact is not generally known.

# CHAPTER VI.

## HOW TO HYPNOTIZE.

In order to correctly and quickly hypnotize a subject, there must be no timidity whatever on the part of the operator. At the start he must manifest the greatest self-confidence and aggressiveness, and such characteristics must not only be manifested, but they must be actually experienced. A false assumption of self-confidence is quickly realized by others and is fatal to the successful performance of hypnotic experiments.

First of all, the operator must determine that to be successful—believing not only that he must not fail, but that he cannot fail. He is about to perform an act that has been performed by others many hundreds of thousands of times. He has studied the philosophy of hypnotism and realizes the nature of what he desires to accomplish. He has learned the methods by which others have hypnotized their subjects. All the precautions have been observed, and therefore success must naturally follow, and will not be due to chance or accident. There is no more uncertainty about it than there is about any of the daily actions of life. These facts the operator must unreservedly realize and not simply believe them in a perfunctory manner.

The labor of producing hypnosis falls upon the operator, and one who attempts the work for the first time is very apt to become wearied by the excitement and nervous strain incident to the unusual mental action. We realize that any severe and unusual physical exercise will tire the muscles and, if carried too far, will produce exhaustion. In a similar manner unusual mental exercise is fatiguing and cannot be indulged in too severely without producing bad effects.

Persons unaccustomed to hypnotizing others must remember these facts while conducting their first experiments. This does not imply that hypnotism is an injurious study and that it is apt to bring about permanent mental exhaustion. It will not produce any more evil effects than any other form of mental labor. How often do we hear of lawyers and ministers and public speakers in general being tired out after some unusual effort. They may be in the habit of speaking in public for an hour at a time with perfect ease, and yet experience the greatest fatigue after half an hour's earnest endeavor to convince doubtful hearers of the truths they wish to impart. It is a species of hypnotism, or mental control, by which a public speaker wins the close attention of his audience and forces the acceptance of his ideas.

There are many methods by which a subject can be hypnotized. These methods differ in particulars, but are essentially the same in principle. The first principle of action is to aim to concentrate the subject's mind upon some one unimportant thought to the exclusion of all others. This thought must, indeed, be so unimportant that when it is the only thought entertained the mind is almost absolutely passive. When this condition is obtained, the second general principle of action may be employed, which consists in making sudden and emphatic suggestions to the passive mind.

### THE FIRST STEP IN PRODUCING HYPNOTISM.

CONCENTRATION OF THOUGHT. — By words and manner the subject must be made to realize that he is about to be hypnotized and that the operator fully understands how and is perfectly able to accomplish the act. The least doubt in the subject's mind in regard to this will render the operator's task more difficult. Don't say, "Now, if I can succeed in hypnotizing you," or "If you are a good subject," or "Perhaps I will not be able to hypnotize you the first time, but I will try." Such expressions destroy all confidence in the operator's ability. Speaking personally, if you indulge in such expression you must expect failure, or at least great difficulty in your attempts.

Make the subject realize the importance and almost solemnity of the occasion. To look upon the performance as a trifling act will be a hindrance. Let him understand that he is to be placed in an unconscious or semi-conscious state and that it means much to him. Create this feeling of awe and the rest of the work will be comparatively easy. If your subject is not in earnest, do not attempt to hypnotize him unless you are an expert, and even then, do not attempt it unless there is some special reason for doing so. You will soon learn to realize quickly the frame of mind of your subject.

Do not for mere self-gratification accept the challenge of anyone who says: "I dare you to hypnotize me." It is a waste of time and energy to trifle with persons who intend to resist your efforts. It is best to turn them off with a laugh, and some such remark as, "Well, if you'll name some future date I'll name the place, and then I will hypnotize you." If he should accept the proposition, select the most quiet and suitable room possible, as described in the chapter on "Influences," and you will be able to hypnotize him or any other person. An insincere person is not apt to accept the proposition, and if he should do so, your self-confidence and his voluntary submission to your conditions will render it easy to hypnotize him.

The concentration of thought, or first step in producing hypnosis, may be accomplished through the medium of any or all of the five senses—sight, hearing, touch, smell, taste. These are of importance in the order named and the impressions made through them must always be continuous and most moderate in degree.

There is no circumstance so well calculated to disturb the subject's mind and prevent hypnosis as attracting his attention to diverse and pronounced objects; while, on the contrary, the greatest aid to hypnosis consists in riveting the attention for a prolonged length of time upon some one object—vague and mysterious in character. Any one of a great variety of objects may be used, some of which will be mentioned.

### OBJECTS USED TO ATTRACT ATTENTION.

The orientals employ various ingenious devises. Among their favorites is a mirror upon which are fastened strips of paper and on these strips of paper are written various characters said to be the names of powerful genii whose influence is to be invoked in producing the desired effect. Upon those who believe in genii and in the powers of the magicians the effect must be very marked, and upon those who are skeptics or absolute unbelievers the result is produced by the sight of the polished surface of the mirror partly concealed by the strips of paper, while the signs, being impossible of interpretations, constitute the mystery.

The Egyptian Sheiks, as a rule, use a polished white plate, upon which various designs and mysterious symbols may be drawn in black ink. While the subject gazes intently upon the plate, he gradually distinguishes darkness in the center, which soon becomes a dark spot and then changes into various fantastic figures. When this occurs he is under hypnotic influence, and so profound a condition of hypnosis can be obtained in subjects who implicitly believe in the operator's powers, that clairvoyant ability is readily manifested.

The fakirs of India sometimes rivet the attention upon snakes which they permit to stupidly move about a circle. They also use jars or dishes into which they pour incense, which, being ignited, produces slowly ascending smoke and an oppressive and not unpleasant odor, at the same time they chant unintelligible words in a monotonous voice. In this manner they employ three of the senses—sight, hearing and smell—all in a modified manner.

Some hypnotists command the subject to stare vacantly into space until a dark spot appears before the eyes, and then to watch that spot develop into various shapes and sizes.

Another plan is to place in the subject's hand a large, glass marble, inside of which has been blown some object. The marble is held at arm's length until the eyes and the arm become weary.

A grotesque Chinese idol was used with great success by a famous operator. The fact of its being an actual idol and its peculiar workmanship rendered it mysterious and valuable.

A bright metal disk, preferably of silver, with a bright, copper button in the center, is used by many. Some believing that the contact of the two metals produces an electric influence that aids hypnosis. But the same effect may result from a disk made of hard black rubber with a circular piece of white or red paper fastened in the center.

A lighted candle, not too brilliant, is sometimes employed by hypnotists. The candle should be held about two feet from the head and just far enough upward to compel the eyes to be held in an unnatural and consequently a tiresome position. Gazing upon this light for about five minutes will greatly aid whatever other efforts are made.

The operator's hands held above the level of the subject's eyes will often answer the purpose of an object to fix the attention upon. Indeed, a great many hypnotists prefer this method, elevating their outstretched arms and allowing the hands to droop from the wrists while the fingers are separated.

Assuming a position close to the subject, the operator with his hands thus placed moves backward six or eight feet, commanding the subject to keep his eyes intently fixed on the fingers. Some subjects will declare that they can experience the magnetism from the tips of the fingers drawing them forward. A slight trembling of the hands will often add to the effectiveness of this method.

The author uses with exceptionally good success a specially contrived instrument. It consists of a black circular disk of polished hard rubber, in the center of which is fastened an artificial eye. The back of the disk is fastened to a small metallic rod about two and a half inches in length and the thickness of an ordinary lead pencil. The subject is instructed to hold this instrument by the small rod, at arm's length, at a height slightly above the level of his head, with the front of the disk facing the subject, who is told to keep his eyes constantly upon the eye on the disk for ten minutes. It seems a long time and is longer than necessary. The operator sits directly in front of the subject in the position mentioned under the heading of "Position of the operator." In about five minutes he says: "Keep your eyes steadily on the disk, but your hand is growing so tired that I will hold the disk for you." This conveys the idea of weariness, which is fully appreciated. Then the subject is told, "Your eyes are growing tired looking so steadily at the disk, wink them if they are tired." In every instance winking quickly commences and the first stage of hypnosis is realized. It is natural next to state that "the eyes are so heavy you can't keep them open," and then they will close and the rest of the performance is comparatively simple.

### THE SENSE OF HEARING.

Next to riveting the attention upon some object through the sense of sight, the use of sound is the most important aid in producing the condition of hypnosis. In fact, very few hypnotists are able to exert complete influence over a subject without in some manner employing this aid.

After the concentration of thought has been at least partially accomplished, then sound is most advantageous. But whatever sounds are made they should always be gentle and monotonous. Discordant sounds will interrupt a hypnotic seance, and intermittent sounds are equally undesirable.

Let us take for example the simplest and most frequent instance of the production of hypnosis—the mother putting her babe to sleep. How soft and soothing is her lullaby, sung in monotonous tones over and over again, with the desire that her babe shall sleep and perfect confidence in her own ability to make it do so.

Oriental magicians, who are expert hypnotists, invariable chant unintelligible words in monotonous tones while placing their subjects under control. Such chanting produces a most desirable drowsiness.

How often have we all been rendered drowsy by the sing-song tones of some public speaker or preacher, and how easy it is for us to go to sleep in church under the influences of such a voice and the otherwise quietude of the situation. With many it is impossible to keep awake under such circumstances. Some preachers, especially among the colored race, take advantage of this power of sing-song preaching to render their listeners pliable to their suggestions without being able to explain how they exercise "such wonderful power." This is often exhibited in colored revival meetings. Persons have come together with the direct purpose of enjoying religious excitement. At first all is quiet expectancy, then the preacher commences his sing-song introduction to his exhortation and continues it until he realizes the receptive state of mind of his hearers, then he "waxes warm," and the sermon commences in earnest. Every word he utters is received just as he desires it to be received. When he makes an unusually good point and wants someone to shout "Amen," or "Glory hallelujah," there is always a response. When he is repeating some pathetic narrative, men and women will groan, and when he expresses fervor, there will be shouts and clapping of hands. So completely are the listeners under control that often the wildest scenes of excitement follow and some assume the condition of catalepsy.

Snake charmers nearly always employ monotonous music or chanting to aid them. It is well known that animals and birds can be thrown into states or ecstasy by repeating over and over again a series of musical sounds. Household dogs will remain undisturbed during the playing of an organ near them, but when a certain pitch of monotonous notes are played, they will instantly rise up and make most agonizing howls. Cats have been known to do the same things, and a donkey may sometimes be made to bray most unmercifully by tooting a horn monotonously in the stable.

After the subject's attention has been sufficiently attracted to secure concentration of thought, then it is the proper time to use the voice for the production of monotonous sounds with implied suggestions. By looking at his eyes the passive condition of his mind can usually be ascertained. He does not appear wide-awake, but has that peculiarly blank stare indicative of distraction from objects and scenes about him. When that expression is recognized, then commence to slowly and in a drawling tone of voice repeat some such sentences as the following:

"You are growing tired. Your eyelids are getting heavy, O, so heavy, you can hardly keep them open. Your eyes are tired, O, so tired, you can't see distinctly. Your head feels heavy. You want to nod. Let your head nod. Your arms are tired, O, so very tired, and so are your legs. They are heavy and you can scarcely move them. Your feet feel like lead. Your whole body is tired. You want to go to sleep. Go to sleep and sleep sound."

Repeat continuously some such words as the above. Do not talk mechanically, but use such a tone of voice as to convey the impression that you, yourself, can scarcely keep awake. Entertain this feeling and you will be able to impart it to the subject.

To subjects who have studied hypnotism to some extent and are subjecting themselves to its influence for the sake of investigation, it will be better to use other language, although the same tone of voice and general manner should be maintained. For instance, say:

"Your mind is passive, your thoughts are all gone. All you can think about is sleep. Your nerves are quiet and now they are resting. Soon you will be asleep. You have no will power left. You will go to sleep in spite of everthing. Sleep is coming."

Of course the intellectual capacity of the subject must always be taken into account, and language used that is suitable to their understanding. Ignorant persons are best influenced by mysterious methods and expressions. They can be overawed. On the other hand, subjects of average intelligence and education do not take kindly to attempts to impress the mysterious upon them. They resent it as a reflection upon their intelligence and feel that the operator does not understand them and therefore cannot hypnotize them. With those who are making a study of the subject, technical expressions are best. They can be led to take the greatest interest in the manoeuvers and methods of procedure and in this manner they will aid their own hypnosis.

In hypnotizing small children, the words conveying the idea of sleepiness can be advantageously sung in a drawling manner. With them, assuring words instead of emphatic statements should be made, and the idea should be conveyed to them that they are feeling good and that it will be very pleasant for them to go to sleep.

### THE SENSE OF TOUCH.

Many persons can be directly hypnotized by the sense of touch, without suggestion or the employment of any other means, and when a subject has been frequently brought under control it will not be difficult to hypnotize him by ommitting the concentration of thought by means of an object of some kind and also by omitting the monotonous and continuous suggestions. Merely touching a subject of this kind will often suffice to throw him into a condition of hypnosis. Still, with an operator with whom he is not acquainted he may prove a most obstinate subject and require the employment of the most impressive methods before he can be influenced.

The production of sleep through the sense of touch is usually spoken of as mesmerism, so-called after Frederick Anton Mesmer, who employed this method (1775) in his experiments that rendered his name famous and laid the foundation for the study of modern hypnotism. His method consisted largely in making passes over the head, face and body, producing what is known as "animal magnetism."

To mesmerize a subject, it is always necessary to have him realize that you intend to put him to sleep through the power of your personal magnetism. In this, as in all other methods of hypnotism, you must first secure the confidence of your subject in your ability, and engender confidence in yourself that you can and will accomplish what you desire.

It is a good plan to rub the fingers together before commencing the operation. It begets a sort of "nervousness" to the tips of the fingers that will produce a tingling sensation when they touch the subject's forehead. This sensation at once convinces him that you are possessed of great magnetic powers. Just how much actual magnetism is developed or how much is necessary, has never been ascertained, but as the expression is convenient, we will employ it.

### THE SENSE OF SMELL.

When it is possible to perform initial hypnotic experiments in a room especially prepared and best adapted to the purpose, it will be found most advantageous to have the room pervaded by some agreeable and indistinct odor. A mixture of faint odors is preferable. Probably the best single odor is that of sandal wood. It produces a drowsy feeling even to those who are not being hypnotized. As it is an odor not familiar to everyone, it is especially useful, for pronounced odors are unfavorable influences.

Never try to hypnotize a person in a room where there is tobacco smoke, and do not allow your breath to be tainted with onions, garlic and similar articles, as disagreeable odors detract the mind and hinder hypnosis.

## THE SENSE OF TASTE.

The eating or drinking by the subject, just before the seance, of anything that will leave a pronounced taste in the mouth, will make hypnosis more difficult. On the other hand, with some persons, especially those who cannot grasp the idea of hypnosis, it is a good plan to give them a very small drink (a brandy glass) of sweetened water containing a few drops of essence of orange and tell them: "This is not a narcotic, it is simply orange water, but it will help you go to sleep." In this way the very delicate flavor of the orange helps to keep up the suggestion of sleep, utilizing the sense of taste for that purpose.

# CHAPTER VII.

## DEGREES OF HYPNOSIS.

Arbitrary division—Power of the operator—Susceptibility of the subject—Drowsiness—Light sleep—Profound sleep—Absolute obedience—Somnambulism—Catalepsy — Lethargy.

The extent to which a person may be placed under hypnotic influence varies according to the character of the individual, the power of the operator, the frequency of hypnosis and other influences.

As a rule, the old cannot be so profoundly influenced as the young, and an operator can have the greater influence over a subject younger than himself, and the more frequent the seances the greater will be the control that may be manifested. An operator who has hypnotized a subject seven or eight times has probably gained as great a control as he can ever exercise over that particular subject as far as the profundity of hypnosis is concerned.

The division of the hypnotic state into various degrees is necessarily somewhat arbitrary, as the transitions from one degree to another are not marked by abruptness. By analogy the division may be compared to the colors of the rainbow—one blending into the other with no absolute dividing lines. Still in the spectrum we recognize seven distinct colors, commencing with the violet and ending with the red, although between these extremes are all conceivable tints and colors.

For all practical purposes, and for the convenience of describing and recording experiments, the following classification of hypnotic phenomena may be accepted:

### FIRST DEGREE—Drowsiness.

The subject realizes and manifests undoubted sleepiness. The eyes seem heavy and he is in the condition of one who is inclined to sleep. Many persons are thrown into this indentical condition by the influence of the quietude of church service and the monotonous voice of a minister preaching a tiresome sermon. He finds it hard work to keep awake, although he realizes all that is said and all that goes on about him. To tell him, in this stage, that he couldn't keep his eyes open, would be to awaken him. Any pronounced command or unfavorable circumstance would quickly destroy the influence obtained, although by favorable influence this degree of hypnosis is easily increased and passes into the next degree.

## SECOND DEGREE—Light Sleep.

There is undoubted evidence of actual sleep with consciousness of what is taking place. The eyes are closed and an emphatic suggestion that they are tight shut will cause the subject to close them very tight, although to dare him to open them might arouse him sufficiently to do so. Nevertheless, in this stage such a statement as "you cannot open your eyes," will usually have the effect of rendering his hypnotic condition more profound. Subjects in this second degree realize everything that is said in their presence, and upon awakening will remember all that was said and done. They may be awakened by unusual noises or by the withdrawal of the operator's presence.

## THIRD DEGREE—Profound Sleep.

The subject will usually droop his head, breathe somewhat heavily and manifest no tendency to awaken. Disturbing influences will not arouse him and the operator may talk to others or withdraw, while the subject will still sleep. Upon suggestion he will open his eyes or if challenged to open them with the remark that he cannot, he will make vain attempts to do so. He will remain in any position suggested that does not require extraordinary effort. Upon awakening he will remember indistinctly all that was said and done.

## FOURTH DEGREE—Absolute Obedience.

In this degree the subject completely loses his

individuality and is a mere automaton in the hands of the operator. He manifests no inclination to falter when commanded to act. He will open and shut his mouth, rotate the hands faster and faster, talk on various topics, make speeches, sing, dance and perform any action that may be ordinarily performed by him while awake, and when 'awakened he will have no recollection of what has taken place.

### FIFTH DEGREE—Somnambulism.

In this state all the senses of the body are under control of the operator, who, by a mere suggestion, may cause the subject to hear, taste, smell, see or experience anything he pleases. It is in this state that anaesthesia or loss of sensation may be produced and the subject rendered capable of withstanding surgical operations. The powers of clairvoyance also belong to this degree, as well as the phenomena of post-suggestion.

### SIXTH DEGREE—Catalepsy.

The production of muscular rigidity characterizes this state. The subject can, by emphatic suggestion, render any or all of his muscles rigid and the whole body may be made "like a piece of stone." It is usual and best that the operator should make frequent passes during catalepsy.

### SEVENTH DEGREE—Lethargy.

There is seldom any occasion for anyone being placed in the lethargic condition, and operators should take the greatest precaution during this dangerous degree. It is, in reality, a semblance of death. The respiration and heart beats are controlled, and the subject may be forced to remain motionless and apparently dead for almost any length of time. Lethargy may be induced during demonstrations for scientific purposes, but its induction for the sake of amusement cannot be too highly condemned.

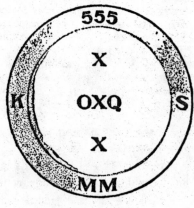

THE PERSIAN PLATE.

# CHAPTER VIII.

## CLAIRVOYANCE.

While in the fifth degree of hypnosis, known as somnambulism, many persons can exercise the power of seeing hidden objects or objects at a great distance. This power is often spoken of as "second sight," and has been known for many centuries. In oriental countries its use is quite frequent and exhibitions of it are made for the entertainment of strangers and as a means of livelihood. In our own land there are many unscrupulous persons pretending to practice clairvoyance who have no knowledge whatever of the art and whose statements are made to credulous persons for the sake of a fee of greater or less proportion, according to the nature of the information furnished.

It is not more than a generation ago since a girdle was put around the earth by means of the electric telegraph and ocean cable and sounds made on one side of the earth were quickly heard upon the other. And it is but a few years ago that we were first enabled to communicate with one another by means of the telephone. Such a proposition would have seemed like a ridiculous fable before its possibility was actually demonstrated. But now we converse with our friends a thousand miles away—our voices being carried along a copper wire under certain conditions, which only those acquainted with electrical apparatus can explain or properly comprehend. Still more incomprehensible to the average person is the marvelous system of wireless telegraphy which is now being so rapidly developed. Nevertheless, we can no longer doubt these methods of communication.

The telephone is, in substance, the prolongation of our nerves of hearing to a distance by means of a wire, at the end of which is an artificial "ear drum," or receiver, to receive the sounds, just as our individual ear drums would receive them. Doubtless, it will not be long before the nerves of sight, as it were, can be prolonged for miles by means of a wire, to transmit the impressions made upon an artificial retina at the end of the line. Such a thing is possible, it is probable, and in fact, we realize that it must soon be a demonstrated reality.

We have no difficulty in realizing in our minds

that wireless telegraphy is conducted by the influence of "currents of electricity through the atmosphere," and we can also realize that its perfection is simply a matter of a short time. To those who have given any thought to these subjects, the power of seeing at a great distance is no more remarkable than wireless telegraphy, and the power of viewing hidden things is no more wonderful than the revelations of the X-rays.

The phenomenon of clairvoyance is in reality the extension, to a greater or less distance, of our powers of observation. In general, the sensations conveyed by our five senses have been confined entirely to things about us and our minds act within a very limited sphere. But it is possible to render our minds perfectly passive and to control the action of our senses so that they may receive impression from objects far removed from our bodies. Our currents of thoughts may bound out into space, utterly disregardless of all physical surroundings, and transmit to our minds conceptions excited at any point toward which our thoughts are propelled.

### CLAIRVOYANCE NOT UNCOMMON.

There are numerous manifestations of this power which have occurred to persons while in profound slumber. Nearly every adult reader can recall experiences where scenes have been witnessed during sleep which were afterward found to be absolute facts which occurred at that time. The author has had many such experiences, one of which will serve to illustrate the subject under discussion.

During the spring of 1884 a great and most devastating flood visited the Ohio valley. The author resided upon one of the hills which surround the city of Cincinnati, remote from the business center. During the night of the highest stage of the flood, he was awakened in the midst of what seemed to be a horrible "nightmare" at first, but which soon appeared as a reality. He awakened the members of the family and explained that he had seen and heard a terrible explosion; that a house had been blown to atoms and that Policeman Macke had been killed and mangled. It was some time before sleep could be restored. Imagine the peculiar sensations conveyed to all when the early morning paper conveyed the information that during the night the occurrence had actually taken place. A man had taken a lighted candle into the cellar of a house six miles away from the author's residence. The cellar was filled with gas caused by the flood backing up the sewers. The gas had exploded and the house had been blown to atoms and Policeman Macke was killed.

This was simply an instance where profound sleep permitted the mind to "wander into space" and receive impressions at a distance as readily as though made close at hand. It is this condition that is called clairvoyance, and it may be produced in some hypnotic subjects without much difficulty.

## HOW TO PRODUCE CLAIRVOYANCE.

To produce clairvoyance, hypnotize the subject by any one of the several methods and gradually cause him to pass from one degree to another until he is profoundly under hypnotic influence in what is termed the somnambulistic state. Make frequent passes from the head downward over the body and test the subject frequently to demonstrate his insensibility to physical sensations when desirable. Then say to him: "You are now a clairvoyant. That is, your mind is able to leave your body and go wherever you wish it to go. You can see whatever you want to you, no matter where it is, and whenever you wish it your mind can come back into your body. I want you to go and look at something for me and tell me all about it. Are you ready?"

### DIRECTING THE CLAIRVOYANT.

When the subject answers, "Yes, I am ready," then proceed to direct him. Not abruptly, but progressively. For instance: If the subject should be in Chicago and it is desired to have him describe a scene in New York, do not say: "Go to New York City and tell me what is going on in my uncle's home." But instead, lead him there as follows: "I want you to go to New York. Now you start out. You are going across the State of Indiana. You are at Indianapolis, but you will not stop there. You are now in Ohio and passing through Columbus on your way to Pittsburg. Now you are crossing Pennsylvania and going over the mountains to Philadelphia. It is a beautiful city and not far from New York. Well, here you are crossing New Jersey. You are at Jersey City, ready to cross the river. At last you are in New York City. It is a great city. You are not going to stop down town. Go up Broadway till you come to Fifty-sixth street. Now, turn east and walk three blocks. There is a large brown house standing all alone, not another house like it on the block. Walk in, you are in the parlor. What do you see?"

By such statements and questions the clairvoyant subject is led on to the desired spot and he will then make his own observations and reply to any questions put to him. If he should hesitate, make more passes and say: "Yes, you can answer."

It may be supposed that the subject is reading the operator's mind and that the operator simply thinks of what he wishes the subject to see or describe. That this is not so, can be readily demonstrated by having a third party name some particular place with which the operator is not familiar, and after being directed to the spot the subject will describe what is to be seen. In many instances news of battles and other important events have been learned through clairvoyance and confirmed by telegraphic reports.

### FINDING HIDDEN OBJECTS.

It is true that an expert clairvoyant can often locate hidden articles, even though they be buried from sight, and many are able to do this through self-hypnotism. This may seem impossible to those who have not seen it practically demonstrated, but without claiming to be clairvoyants many persons have been able to locate lost articles through visions that came to them during natural sleep. Profound sleep is a self-induced hypnotic condition, and in some persons it amounts to the condition known as somnambulism, in which state clairvoyance is possible.

The gift of second sight was formerly more generally recognized than it is at the present day, probably because so many charlatans and imposters monopolize the "business," and use their powers (if they possess any) to convince people of their assumed ability to correctly read the future.

Young subjects usually make the best clairvoyants, especially those of a dreamy nature. The possibilities that present themselves through this branch of hypnotism are very great, and the spirit of investigation which permeates the scientific world, will prompt discoveries and experiments that will demonstrate the great benefits to be derived from the practice of true clairvoyance.

# CHAPTER IX.

## SELF-HYPNOTISM—AUTO-SUGGESTION.

We all possess the power of self-hypnotization. It
is a natural endowment that is capable of being
developed for much good. To a certain extent we
unconsciously take advantage of this power at many
times without creating in ourselves or others the
least cause for wonderment.

If you should retire at night with the intention of
awakening at four o'clock in order to catch a five
o'clock train, and should impress upon your mind
most emphatically the necessity of your awakening
at the desired time, you would be pretty sure to find
yourself wide awake at four o'clock. Many persons

cultivate this control over the mind and can easily awaken themselves at any moment they may decide upon before going to sleep. It is a very useful form of self-hypnotism.

By the same process it is possible to cultivate most exact habits of promptness in keeping appointments. Simply train yourself to fix in your mind where you have agreed to be at a certain time and when that time arrives you will be involuntarily prompted to keep the appointment. Some persons will even find themselves hurriedly walking in a certain direction and have no recollection when they start out what place they intended to go to, but before going far the full particulars come to them. These are instances where the time and direction weere impressed upon the mind and the idea transferred to the seat of physical action.

In the city of Cincinnati there formerly resided a blind man who sold papers upon the street corner. By some unaccountable method he had trained himself to fix in his mind the time of day. No matter what the hour might be, whenever he was asked for the time he would give it with the greatest exactness.

### GOING TO SLEEP.

In the matter to going to sleep we perform the act of self-hypnotism and without any thought of this fact we place ourselves under the influences most favorable to hypnosis and yield to them. We seek quietude and the most comfortable position possible and then we strive to render our minds passive and to concentrate the thought upon only one idea and that is the idea of sleep. Practice has convinced us that we will go to sleep under such circumstances and we are accordingly overcome by self-hypnosis. Unfavorable influences may keep us awake, just as they may prevent the subject from being hypnotized by the operator.

It is an excellent plan to cultivate the habit of self-hypnotism to the degree of being able to go to sleep at any moment desired. Prof. O. S. Fowler, the noted phrenologist, declared that in the midst of a public demonstration he would frequently excuse himself for a short intermission, when someone else would entertain the audience, and, retiring to an ante-room, he would sink into a chair and quickly force himself to sleep for a few minutes. This sleep would refresh him wonderfully and he would reappear upon the stage with renewed vigor, to finish his demonstrations and lecture in a most vivacious manner.

### HOW TO PRODUCE SELF-HYPNOSIS.

The production of self-hypnosis can be easily cultivated by anyone of determined will and ordinary intelligence. First choose the best surroundings obtainable, as mentioned in the chapter on Influences. Select a quiet room where noise from the street and the rest of the house cannot be heard or where they will be least heard. Have the room dimly lighted and if possible let it be scented by the odor of flowers or delicate perfume. Lie down in the most comfortable position possible, making sure that the light does not shine in the eyes. Relax every muscle of the body, that is, let the muscles feel perfectly listless, as though they had no power or strength in them. Fix the sight upon some object a short distance from the body in such a position that the eyes will be compelled to look slightly upward. Look steadfastly at this object and do not allow the eyes for an instant to look at anything else. Do not wink or shut the eyes until it is absolutely impossible to keep them open. Breathe slowly and regularly, and do not think of your breathing beyond the thought that this slow and regular breathing is producing sleep. Concentrate your mind altogether upon the one thought of sleep and that by looking at the object without faltering and breathing regularly and slowly you are gradually becoming unconscious. You will go to sleep.

As you put yourself to sleep let it be with the thought that at a certain time you will awaken. Convince yourself that you will sleep soundly during ten minutes or an hour or ten hours or ten days or ten weeks. When you have complete control over yourself in producing self-hypnosis, you can decide upon any length of time your sleep will endure and you will not awaken until that time has elapsed. If you do not establish a certain time for awakening you can usually be aroused by others or by disturbances, such as would arouse any sound sleeper.

Some of the orientals force themselves to sleep with the positive auto-suggestion to sleep during a period of six months or years without any one being able to awaken them. They sleep during the selected time as though they were in a trance (which is the fact) or as though they were absolutely dead.

It is claimed by the relatives of Bishop, the great mind reader, that his apparent death was simply a trance-like condition into which he had thrown himself. Physicians finding him apparently dead, seized upon the opportunity to hold a post-mortem for the purpose of examining his brain, and it is claimed that his actual death was caused by the knives of these would-be investigators. The truthfulness of the claim can never be proven, but the relatives can never be convinced that he was not murdered in the interests of science while in a trance.

The following item is clipped from a daily newspaper of recent date and is decidedly interesting in this connection:

HYPNOTIZES HIMSELF WHILE AT CHURCH.

Young Man Frightens Friends and Keeps Physicians Busy
for Some Time.

"Clinton, Iowa, May 4.—Lindsay Smith of this city has aroused some curiosity by hypnotizing himself. For the benefit of some unbelieving friends he placed himself under self-hypnotic influence while attending the Methodist Church.

"Several of the women who saw his protruding eyes and rigid form screamed, and physicians were called to work with the young man. It was some time before he was aroused.

"He is afraid to repeat the operation for fear of being unable to arouse himself."

The production of profound sleep for a great length of time by self-hypnotism is not advisable. Not that there is any real danger incurred, but because it is very apt to excite alarm in others and cause fright and possibly bring reproach upon the science and practice of hypnotism.

### DISEASE BY SELF-HYPNOTISM.

It is a well-known fact that a person can so completely concentrate his thoughts upon his liability to sickness that the least suggestion will produce in him all the discomforts of actual disease and not infrequently the disease itself.

Persons who, during a small-pox epidemic, are in constant dread of "catching" the disease, are extremely liable to cantract it upon exposure. Abundant proof of this has been furnished. The mind has been so concentrated upon the subject and upon the symptoms of the disease that there exists no longer any resistive powers.

By constantly believing that they have heart disease, many persons cause the heart to beat irregularly and to palpitate. Some can readily control the heart's action and make it beat at pleasure anywhere from thirty to two hundred times a minute. A gentleman, who was once refused insurance on account of a heart beat of over one hundred per minute on several occasions, practiced the method of auto-suggestion and was enabled to regulate his heart pulsations to seventy-five per minute while undergoing a subsequent examination. This regulation of the heart causes amusement to many, but its common practice is unadvisable, for the reason that it is never beneficial to force any of the organs of the body to perform their functions in a manner that is not physiological. Care must be taken in all hypnotic experiments to avoid anything that will injure or weaken the body.

The power of imagination is capable of doing great harm. Persons who have little to do in this life are very apt to concentrate their thoughts entirely upon themselves and in that manner make themselves liable to be affected by the least suggestions of bodily ailments. The hypochondriac is an example of self-hypnotism. He suggests to himself the possibility of his being affected by various diseases of the internal organs—heart disease being a general favorite. By studying the symptoms of these various diseases he soon convinces himself that he experiences them all, and in most cases actually does suffer the pains he imagines.

This is occasioned in precisely the same manner that a hypnotized subject may be made to believe, by the suggestions of the operator, that he is warm or cold or wet or suffering. The only difference is that in the case of self-hypnotism the sufferer is the operator and subject combined in one.

An illustrative case of auto-suggestion has recently been brought to the notice of the students attending the clinic of Prof. L. D. Rogers. A gentleman, who had most probably exposed himself to the contact of disease, presented himself for treatment of a possible infection. He was thoroughly examined and no evidence whatever found to indicate the least pathological condition. He contended that he had nearly all the symptoms of the difficulty feared and believed that by some accident he had contracted it. Here was clearly a case of imagination, based upon undoubted exposure. Fear had concentrated the mind upon the single thought of contracting the disease and the suffering was consequently experienced, although there was no physical evidence of wrong. After due consultation, held before the patient, it was decided to give him "No. 79," a name given a placebo, or simple water, supposed to be a solution of some powerful drug. The strong character of the preparation was impressed upon the patient and he was given directions how to use it. A few days afterward he returned to the clinic greatly improved, but still suffering from some of the symptoms he imagined. It was decided in his presence to give him a "much stronger preparation," called "No. 97," which was to be taken with great exactness. This preparation was in reality nothing but distilled water, but nevertheless it had the desired effect.

### IMAGINARY SKILL AND ABILITY.

The constant dwelling of the mind upon any one subject is very apt to produce a concentration of thought that results in self-hypnotism. Some persons invent wonderful tales of what occurred to them on hunting or fishing expeditions and repeat their stories over and over again so frequently that they finally actually believe in their truthfulness, although in reality knowing they are mere fabrications.

A certain gentleman of liberal income, obtained through questionable methods, became possessed of the idea that he would like to become famous as an author. He could not write an ordinary letter correctly and had no knowledge whatever of the subjects upon which he desired others to think him an authority. He thereupon paid gentlemen of literary attainments a meager sum for writing books for him. These books he had printed with his own name upon the title page as author. They met with a ready sale and he was frequently quoted by various writers who had never met him, and who were not acquainted with the facts. His acquaintances, however, quickly realized his bogus authorship and took delight in carrying on conversations with him upon various topics treated in his books, laughing to themselves at his crude opinions that were at such variance with those printed under his name. But the constant reference to him as an author impressed itself deeply upon his mind, until he grew to actually experience a "realizing sense" of his ability, and finally became convinced that he had exhausted his nervous system by too much brain work expended in writing his books. He would expatiate upon his many months of arduous literary labor in the midst of business, and do it with such sincerity that friends began to realize that he labored under a mental delusion. He had simply hypnotized himself, and as there is no counteracting influence, his condition will probably remain unchanged until some one rudely awakens him to the fact that his bogus authorship is generally known, and that he has long been a "laughing stock" to many on account of it.

Such incidents in various lines are common. A manufacturer, who had secured over a thousand patents on contrivances devised by his employes, became convinced that he was one of the greatest inventors of the age and was made an officer in the Society of Inventors, although the only work he had ever done in that line was to invent methods of securing, without remuneration, the results of the genius of his employes.

### ADVANTAGES OF SELF-HYPNOTISM.

Self-hypnotism is a most interesting study and the benefits to be derived from auto-suggestion are numerous. It is a good plan to realize that we possess such power within ourselves and to cultivate its use.

During sickness it will enable us to turn our minds away from our sufferings and expedite recovery. During bereavement it will help us turn our minds to other things. With all due reverence to religious beliefs, it can be positively stated that it is this power that sustains devout persons when troubles come upon them. They are able to concentrate their thoughts upon Him whom they worship and thus throw off their sorrows. It is a scriptural doctrine that belief and faith are essentials to perfect peace. The absolute belief that all sins have been taken away from them has been a source of great joy to many who were before miserable in life because of the constant recollection of their misdeeds. Belief that they will be Divinely protected from harm enables many to fearlessly, and without injury, run risks of contagion and deprivation and exposure that would certainly seriously affect others who had no power or method of controlling their fears.

# CHAPTER X.

## ACCIDENTAL DEVELOPMENT OF HYPNOTIC POWER.

Case of Gertrude Pennington—Playing while asleep—Case of
Mr. Charles Gardner—Put the baby to sleep—Couldn't
wake the baby—Mothers naturally hypnotize their babies
—Case of Marguerite McAllister—Hypnotizing restless patients—The crucifix used to concentrate the thoughts.

Very many persons realize their hypnotic powers
by accident, and are unable to even attempt to
explain their actions. Not infrequent cases of children
exhibiting marvelous powers of this kind have been
reported, and they manifestly performed their work
without giving thought of how they did it.

### CASE OF GERTRUDE PENNINGTON.

Gertrude Pennington, of Pennsylvania, born and
reared in the mountains, with but few companions
and most meager conditions for mental development,
was, by accident, observed to possess the most
remarkable hypnotic powers, which her parents had
never before known to be possible to anyone, having
never heard of hypnotism in any form. One day her
father, while working in the barnyard, noticed his

four children and three others enter the barn. They remained for some time and for awhile he could hear their noise made in romping and playing games. Suddenly all became quiet and remained so for so long a time that he became alarmed lest some accident had befallen them. He entered the barn, and climbing quietly to the loft, he was so amazed at what he saw before him that he stood motionless for some time before demanding an explanation.

Gertrude, fourteen years old, the oldest of the children, stood erect with hands outstretched toward the others, who were lying in various positions in a deep sleep. She frequently repeated the words, "Sleep, children, sleep." After awhile she said: "It is time to get up." They all arose and made motions as though they were dressing and then washing their faces and combing the hair. Then she told them, "Breakfast's ready," and they sat down around a large box and acted precisely as though they were eating a hearty meal.

Mr. Pennington could not restrain his curiosity any longer and made his presence known by exclaiming: "What on earth are you children doing?" Gertrude at once cried out in a shrill voice: "Children, stop it, stop it," and loudly clapped her hands. The others seemed startled, stopped their imaginary meal, and assumed an air of guilty sheepishness. Gertrude then said to her father, "We were only playing, we won't do it again."

This unusual form of play and their evident discomfiture at being discovered, led to the father and mother both making investigations and doing a great deal of questioning, from which they found out that for some time Gertrude had been "playing" this way with the children, and that they stood in great awe of her in consequence. Sometimes she would let one or another watch the others act, and those who performed their parts declared they did not know what they were doing after Gertrude put them to sleep. They called their sport "playing in our sleep." Mr. Pennington did not fancy this kind of play and ordered them to "never do it again," but nevertheless he had frequent occasions afterward to punish Gertrude for disobedience on this account. She enjoyed the play and so did the children and at a mere nod and suggestion they would follow her to some secluded spot to "play in our sleep."

### CASE OF CHARLES GARDINER.

Another instance of the accidental discovery of hypnotic power was the case of Mr. Charles Gardiner, living in a suburb of Cincinnati. He and his wife had planned to attend an evening entertainment, and before leaving the house Mrs. Gardiner attempted to put to sleep their three-year-old child, that the older children would not be bothered by doing so. Being in a hurry and consequently nervous, she failed in her efforts and the child got in a state frequently known as the "tantrums," and resisted all efforts made to quiet her. Mr. Gardiner became quite angry at the noise and delay and seizing the child said: "Here, I'll put her to sleep." He held the child at arm's length and shook her and commanded her in very forcible terms to "go to sleep and stay to sleep till I tell you to wake up." She went to sleep, and did so with such suddenness that both father and mother feared something was wrong. They laid her in the crib, watched her breathing for awhile, noting that it was all right, and then left. The child slept soundly all night and was sleeping when Mr. Gardiner left for business next morning. About 11 o'clock he was summoned home by the message that "We can't wake up the baby." At the same time the family physician had been sent for and had vainly expended his efforts before Mr. Gardiner arrived, and being told the circumstances of the previous evening he declared it a clear case of hypnotic sleep. As soon as the father entered the room he took the child in his arms and said: "Baby, wake up, quick, wake up," and in an instant the child was awake, perfectly sound and well. The incident, for awhile, caused a great shock, but it revealed to Mr. Gardiner his hypnotic powers, which he afterward utilized in various ways.

It may not be generally so considered, but it is a fact that the putting to sleep of infants is usually a species of hypnotism, the monotonous lullaby of the mother and her quiet determination to produce sleep being but the usual method of producing hypnosis from which the child in time naturally awakens, because it is not profound.

## CASE OF MARGUERITE M'ALISTER.

Miss Marguerite McAlister, of Chicago, for years had a great reputation for being a most successful nurse, and commanded the highest salary for her services. She was often spoken of as a woman who had a peculiarly soothing influence over patients. She privately informed me that her success lay almost altogether in her hypnotic ability which she had discovered by accident in a peculiar manner, and she had kept her secret to herself, lest persons might object to her on account of it.

At one time she had for a patient a very sensitive and irritable young woman suffering from a broken leg. This caused her to worry greatly about her work, she being a school teacher and fearful lest she should lose her position. The worry caused loss of sleep for several nights and threatened to bring on brain fever from insomnia and exhaustion. Miss McAlister tells the story in these words:

"My patient was a devout Catholic, and one night after every effort to quiet her and induce natural sleep had failed, I suddenly decided to try to affect her through her faith in religion. I picked up a little crucifix and fastened it to the bed post at the foot of the bed and told her to look at it steadily for ten minutes and to think of nothing but that her Savior would allow her to go to sleep. I kept my watch in my hand to notice when the ten minutes should be up. She kept her eyes on the crucifix steadily throughout the whole time and at the end of ten minutes I said: 'Now, shut your eyes and you'll go to sleep.' I no sooner said it than her eyes closed tightly and she slept soundly all night. I had no thought of hypnotizing her when I commenced, but I soon realized what had been done, for I had read a great deal on the subject. The next night I repeated the experiment and when the ten minutes of looking at the crucifix had expired I said: 'Now, you are going to sleep, and after this, every night that you look at the crucifix this way you will have a good night's rest,' and so she did."

Miss McAlister said that when she had Catholics for patients she always used the crucifix in this way when they were sleepless, and it always brought about the desired effect. With others, she would call their attention to some object for the required space of time, telling them that such a plan had always brought sleep to restless persons she had nursed, and sleep was sure to follow under the com·bined influence of their steady gaze and her emphatic assurance and her hypnotic influence, which she cul·tivated with much earnestness, taking pains to keep all thoughts of hypnotism from her patrons, lest prejudice might injure her reputation as a successful nurse. Happily such prejudice is fast giving away to public approval of such methods.

# CHAPTER XI.

## THE HYPNOTIST'S SECRET.

Unpublished facts—How hypnotic power is developed—Focusing the mind—Forcing subjection—Expelling thoughts—Overcoming the subject's resistance—Practicing on dummies—Useless efforts—Practicing self-control—Increasing hypnotic power—Realizing individual influence—Overcoming individual habits—Curing personal disorders—Making friends — Overpowering enemies—Forestalling events—Sphere of hypnotic influence.

There are important facts in connection with hypnotism that have never yet been published. These are usually considered the secrets of hypnotists that must be taught by the teacher to his pupil or learned by experience. That a knowledge of them is absolutely necessary for the successful production of the various degrees of hypnosis will be realized by all who undertake the practice of hypnotism.

The most important knowledge to be obtained in this connection is how to develop hypnotic power. The student may realize that he possesses this power in a dormant state and may experience a sensation as though he were being restrained by some invisible force from exercising this hypnotic power, which seems to be confined within him like a mental prisoner. When such feelings are experienced it is indisputable evidence of hypnotic ability which should be developed. After reading the chapters on "Qualifications of a Hypnotist" and "How to Hypnotize," the student should train himself by the following method while experimenting with a subject:

FOCUSING THE MIND.—Conceive the mind to be an accumulation of nerve force in the brain and the eyes to be the exit. In imagination realize a mythical lens before the eyes through which the nerve force must pass and endeavor to so adjust the imaginary lens that the "rays" of nerve force shall focus in the mind of the subject. All thoughts must be banished from the mind except the one thought of influencing the subject. Let this thought go out in a direct line to penetrate his mind. This method of focusing the mind can be practiced in seclusion without the presence of a subject. It calls for the exercise of imagination, but without imagination hypnotism is difficult to master.

FORCING SUBJECTION.—Constantly endeavor to exert an influence over others by your will power. Learn to control by thought and desire and not by words. It is surprising to realize how well you can make your wishes known by simply "throwing out thoughts." Do this upon all occasions. When you wish to attract the attention of someone in the room with you, will that he shall turn about and look at you. When you desire anything at the table, mentally ask for it and you will soon be asked if you desire it. Practice will show you remarkable instances of others feeling your mental demands.

When you have a subject before you, devote all your mental energy to compelling his subjection to your influence. Do not only desire that he shall obey you or hope that you may be able to influence him, but entertain no shadow of doubt of your ability to control him. Mentally force him to obey your suggestions with as much confidence as you would feel in verbally commanding a child.

EXPELLING THOUGHTS.—A passive mind is the first requisite of a good subject, and a good operator must likewise be able to make his own mind passive before he can concentrate his thoughts sufficiently to control others. Continually practice making the mind passive in the same manner that you would employ in driving thoughts from your mind when endeavoring to get to sleep at night when inclined to stay awake. Simply entertain no thought. It is a good plan to seat yourself in a comfortable position and stare vacantly into space for several minutes at a time. Looking at a blank wall or a mirror too high to show your own reflection, will often aid the expulsion of thought. Make your mind a blank very frequently. This is one of the best methods of gaining complete control over your mental powers.

OVERCOMING RESISTANCES.—At times your subject will seemingly resist your most arduous efforts to

control him. It may seem to you that your nerve
force, thrown out from your mind, is striking against
a stone wall. In such a case, do not abandon your
effort if you have ever before hypnotized the subject.
Make your mind passive as possible for a short time
while the subject is before you. This will mentally
throw him off his guard. Then suddenly concentrate
your thoughts upon the one idea of overcoming his
resistance, focus your mind, and make the attack
successfully.

DUMMIES. —A large bolster or pillow, propped up
in a chair, will serve as a dummy upon which to
practice position and other hypnotic efforts. This
may seem to be absurd, but it can be done with great
benefit. Of course it takes considerable exercise of
imagination; but the imagination must be frequently
exercised in the practice of hypnotism.

USEFUL EFFORTS.—There are times when every
effort of a beginner to hypnotize a subject meets with
failure, even under the most favorable extraneous
conditions, on account of mental or physical peculiarities of the subject practiced upon. The expert
hypnotist quickly detects such peculiarities almost
by intuition. It is important to realize the probability
of failure in time to avoid useless effort, for arduous
endeavors to hypnotize a subject, followed by failure,
always weakens the operator and diminishes his
ability to quickly hypnotize others.

To maintain confidence in your own hypnotic
ability is of vital importance, and for that reason

never concede defeat, even to yourself. If you entertain any feelings of doubt concerning your ability to hypnotize any particular subject, do not attempt to do so. If, after commencing the sitting you become conscious of timidity upon your part or realize the subject's stubborn resistance, quickly make your mind passive, as mentioned in the paragraph on overcoming resistance, and then make one short effort. If you realize your timidity has disappeared and that the subject is weakening, proceed and you will be successful. If you do not realize these things, abandon the attempt with the statement to the subject that you must postpone the sitting until he is in another frame of mind.

PRACTICE SELF-CONTROL—If you cannot control yourself you must not expect to control others. Persons who are unable to exclude unpleasant thoughts or to keep their minds upon one thing at a time cannot become good hypnotists. Cultivate the habit of driving from your mind every thought that is not directly connected with the work you are performing. Let this be your constant habit, even in the most trivial matters. If you are upon a pleasure trip or at an entertainment of any kind, let only self-enjoyment in what is taking place be your aim. Positively exclude thoughts of business or domestic matters when you are not participating in those duties of life, and when attending to business, think of nothing else. Concentration of thought is the keynote of success in hypnotism.

One of the greatest secrets of the development of hypnotic power is the practice of instantly falling to sleep as soon as your head touches the pillow. When you retire for the night, banish every thought from your mind, except the thought of going to sleep. Force yourself to sleep by making your mind a blank to every idea except that of sleep. When you have yourself under perfect control in this particular, you will realize your hypnotic ability and be able to make others realize it. You must have the power to go to sleep whenever you will to do so, no matter what may be your surroundings.

INCREASING HYPNOTIC POWER —Beginners often suppose that in order to increase their hypnotic power they should practice upon as many subjects as possible. The reverse of this is true, for inexperienced operators are sure to meet with many failures, and that means loss of self-confidence. First secure a good subject and practice upon him until you can hypnotize him with absolutely no difficulty and then place him in the profound stages of hypnosis, although lethargy should not be produced. Next, secure two or three more subjects and develop them, and thus gradually add to the number.

It is poor policy for even an expert to be promiscuous in choosing subjects. Be careful in your selections and do not grant every request to "hypnotize someone." Confine yourself strictly to business and always have a reason for placing anyone in the hypnotic state, even though that reason should be simply your own development of power. Never make hypnotism a trivial matter. While great amusement can be afforded others at the expense of your subjects, you should avoid making a mountebank of yourself. Let everyone realize the importance of the power you are able to display and realize that importance yourself. In this way you preserve your dignity and increase your hypnotic ability, which would by any other course be likely to diminish.

REALIZING INDIVIDUAL INFLUENCE —Notice among your friends which ones pay you respect, not only for the sake of politeness, but for your own sake. Notice what percentage of persons are actually interested in what you say and are willing to check their own desire to speak when you commence to talk. Cultivate the manners of acting and talking that will increase the number of persons you can influence. It is surprising how quickly you can increase the number by making a habit of looking everyone in the eye to whom you speak and by developing self-confidence. Commence by choosing subjects of conversation that will interest others and by making remarks that are of personal interest to them. This method will cause you to realize that attention is being paid to your words and will accustom you to being a speaker rather than a listener. It is then that your individual influence over others will be realized and the cultivation of it will become easy.

OVERCOMING INDIVIDUAL HABITS.—A bad habit is always a species of slavery, and a slave makes a good hypnotic subject, but a poor operator. A student of hypnotism cannot make a better beginning than by overcoming his own bad habits. He must be able to influence his own thoughts and actions by the exercise of will power. If he cannot do so, he will hardly be able to overcome the individual will power of others.

CURING PERSONAL DISORDERS.—A good hypnotist must have a sound body. Dyspepsia, indigestion, constipation, neuralgia and all other complaints, must be cured. By curing them is not meant overcoming them by narcotics, poisons, harsh cathartics, artificial digestants, etc. Such things are poor excuses for medicines. They may, indeed, force various organs to act or destroy the sensitive powers of the nerves, but they weaken the body. Avoid poisons and narcotics. There are hundreds of harmless agents that can be used to aid natural efforts toward restoring health; and in addition, pure air, pure water, exercise and cheerfulness will work wonders in the way of curing personal disorders. Invalids should not attempt to become hypnotists, they should rather pose as subjects.

MAKING FRIENDS.—Cultivate the habit of inspiring cheerfulness in others. Make your presence desirable and refrain from going where you are not wanted. Such a practice will give you an air of freedom that will aid you in developing hypnotic power. There is no restraint among friends, and the more friends you have about you the more accustomed you will become to being free from self-consciousness, which is fatal to hypnotic success.

OVERPOWERING ENEMIES .—Anyone possessing individuality will surely have enemies, but let the hypnotist beware of falling into the hands of his enemies. Avoid defeat, for it lowers your own estimation of your individual power. Keep yourself from entanglements with others that might terminate disastrously. If you can overpower your enemies by cool judgment or refraining from disputes you have increased your self-possession and power.

FORESTALLING EVENTS—It is a wise man who can foresee evil and prepare to successfully meet it. Make a habit of looking far ahead in everything you undertake, so as to be ready for any emergency that may arise. Such a habit will give you tranquility of mind and self-confidence. It will engender in you a feeling that you can overcome difficulties whenever they arise. It is that state of mind that favors hypnotic power.

SPHERE OF HYPNOTIC INFLUENCE.—The beginner's sphere of hypnotic influence is small, but the expert hypnotist can influence nearly everyone with whom he comes in contact. It is important to continually strive, in daily life, to influence others for good. Realizing that your influence has induced action will increase your desire to control others, and this will increase your power to do so. After you have successfully hypnotized several subjects, you should constantly endeavor to turn your power to good use, for the more good you can be the means of accomplishing, the wider will become your sphere of hypnotic influence.

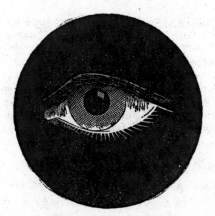

THE AUTHOR'S DISK.

# CHAPTER XII.

## DEVELOPING A SUBJECT.

Beginners in the practice of hypnotism often make the great mistake of attempting too much at the first seance. When they realize that they have actually hypnotized a subject, they usually become somewhat excited and are very apt to try to accomplish everything at once. Expert operators, under favorable circumstances, can sometimes force a new subject through all the degrees of hypnotism during the first seance, but such a performance should not be attempted by beginners. It involves a great deal of labor and is tiresome to the operator and exceedingly likely to fail, and failure means discouragement and a

consequent loss of self-confidence.  Do not expect
too much and you will not be disappointed.

After you have thoroughly studied the principles
of hypnotism and convinced yourself of your ability
to produce hypnosis, then look about you for a suitable subject upon which to practice.  In choosing
a subject for your first experiments, several things
must be considered, for a great deal depends upon
your first efforts proving successful.

### CHOOSING A SUBJECT.

Always select a subject whom you know to be
capable of being influenced by you—someone you
would not hesitate to command, someone who looks
up to you and shows in an unmistakable manner that
he considers you to be his mental superior.  It may
take some time to find just such a person who is also
willing to subject himself to your influence, but do
not commence your experiments until he is found.

Many may express their willingness to allow you
to try to hypnotize them, and may be sincere in
their desire to aid you, but such persons, as a rule,
impress you with a sense of willingness that amounts
to condescension on their part andd places you in
the position of receiving a favor, which is a fatal position for a beginner in hypnotism to occupy.

Never undertake to practice upon anyone who
excites in you a feeling of awe or superiority, or one
whom you know to be better educated than yourself
or one who occupies a social or business position

that causes you to pay him deference. For if you realize inferiority in any respect, you cannot assert the air of superior power that is absolutely necessary to the successful hypnotist.

Having selected a subject that accords with your idea, it is a good plan to lead him gradually to submission. Incidentally tell him of your hypnotic knowledge and relate experiences of others and assert boldly that you have been studying the science and have developed hypnotic power. Do not let him know he is your first subject. Then dare him to let you hypnotize him. It is best to commence on some young man about sixteen years of age, who is accustomed to working under a hard boss for little pay. He is accustomed to obedience and will be glad of a chance to become conspicuous and can easily be induced to submit himself by promising him a quarter or half dollar for being hypnotized. "No hypnotism, no pay," will urge him to carefully obey instructions.

### THE FIRST SEANCE.

After you have obtained the consent of a proper subject, do not undertake to experiment with him in the presence of by-standers, but make some private arrangements with him and as far as possible secure the influences named in Chapter IV. It is not supposed that a beginner can have everything in his favor, but many of the favorable influences can be provided—quietude being by far the most essential.

Speak to your subject in some such manner as

follows: "As this is the first time you have been hypnotized, I will promise you not to put you very sound to sleep. First, I will not put you to sleep at all, but I will find out how easily you can be influenced."

Have him stand up in front of you. Place your hands upon his shoulders and stare into his eyes and ask him to look straight at you. By his expression you will soon realize that he is subservient. Keep staring into his eyes until the stare becomes tiresome and moisture is seen in his eyes, then suddenly relieve the silence by saying: "You're all right. I can hypnotize you without any trouble. Now, sit down in this chair, put your feet close together, take this disk in your right hand, hold it at arm's length and look at it steadily."

Speak to him in a manner that conveys to his mind that you are thorough master of the situation, that you are perfectly familiar with every detail and that there is no element of doubt anywhere. The fact that he will readily do just as you tell him to do is the accomplishment of the first step toward hypnosis. You are the operator; he is the subject. You are commanding; he is obeying. Satisfactory results must follow.

After he has steadily held for five minutes and gazed at the disk, or any article similar to those named in Chapter VI, seat yourself quietly in front of him, place one hand on top of his upon his knee and with the other take from him the disk, saying: "I'll take this now; your arm is getting tired. Keep

looking at it steadily till your eyes get tired, too.
Now they're getting tired. Wink them if you want
to. Shut them. That's it. Now you're drowsy,
very drowsy. Go to sleep. Go to sleep. Keep your
eyes tight shut. Go to sleep."

The subject will go to sleep. Perhaps not fully.
He may smile and almost lead you to think he is
shamming. He knows what you are saying and
doing. What if he does? He is obeying you and
will obey you still more. Don't make a sudden
demand upon him, but gradually lead him onward.

Make passes over the head, from the back forward.
Keep telling him to sleep and sleep soundly. Use a
drawling tone of voice and enter into the spirit of
drowsiness. Keep him in this condition at least ten
minutes. If he should suddenly awaken, show no
discomfiture, but quickly say: "Well, that's enough
for to-day. You're a good subject, and we will do
this again soon; only next time we will go a little
farther."

The chances are that the subject will not awaken
of his own accord, especially if you say to him:
"Sleep till I tell you to wake up." He may be perfectly conscious and yet will manifest his drowsiness
in an unmistakable manner. In that case, carry the
experiment a little farther and make some farther
suggestion. For instance: "Your eyes are so tightly
closed that you can't open them. Shut them tighter,
tighter, tight shut. Now, you can't open them.
Shut them tight." He will shut his eyes very tight

and then make an attempt to open them, which you must not encourage, lest he should succeed. Tell him: "Never mind, now sleep," and then make passes as before and let him become drowsy and remain so for some time and then snap your fingers and say: "All right! wake up. You're all right."

He will quickly awaken and look confused for awhile and perhaps remark: "Is that all? Why, I knew all the time what you were doing." Tell him: "Certainly you did. I told you I wouldn't hypnotize you very soundly. Next time we will do more." This gains his confidence. He realizes he obeyed you and that you did in fact hypnotize him, and stopped because you did not care to do more. It is well also to tell him that the operation tired you, which will be the truth, for your nerve tension and suppressed excitement is exhausting.

## THE SECOND SEANCE.

During your second seance you can accomplish much more. After proceeding as before, make suggestions to him that will call his attention to sensations about the head or upper part of the body or cause him to employ his hands. For example:

"You are perspiring on your forehead. Take your hand and wipe off the perspiration." He will do so. "Loosen your collar and wipe off your neck." "There is a little bug back of your ear. Your head itches. Scratch it. You are perspiring again. Wipe the perspiration from your forehead. Your hands are wet with it. Rub your hands together. Make your hands go like a wheel. Round and round and round. Faster, faster, faster, faster. Now the other way. Now back again. Now the other way. Now stop them."

All your suggestions will be instantly carried out, and your mind may think of a great many diverse actions that will require movements of the hands, without involving the lower part of the body. It may be probable that during the second seance, the most profound hypnosis can be produced, but it is best not to attempt more than has been mentioned at this time.

### THE THIRD SEANCE.

The third time you place the subject under your hypnotic influence, you can go to great extremes with safety and perfect confidence.

He will not open his eyes until you tell him to do so and it is best for him to keep them shut during the performances of at least the first, second and third experiments. The third trial will be best adapted to muscular suggestions.

Make passes over the forehead and press the thumb between the eyes and tell him: "You can't open your eyes, try it, you can't do it." He will try in vain. Then say: "Now you can open them, but shut them again." Make passes from his shoulders to his wrists and tell him to fasten his hands together and that he can't take them apart. After he has struggled in vain to do so. tell him: "Now, you can take them apart." Make passes from his head to his knees and tell him he can't get off the chair. Then tell him: "Now, you can get up." After he is up you can make him dance or walk or stand immovable or do almost anything that is not dangerous or ridiculous. It is best not to suggest anything laughable until the fourth experiment. Just before ending the third seance say: "Now, stay asleep, but open your eyes. Look at me steadily and when I count three, then wake up." Count three and then say loudly: "All right. Wake up; wake up. You're all right."

### THE FOURTH SEANCE.

The fourth seance may be characterized by the full limit of hypnosis, but it is best to confine it to the production of somnambulism. After repeating the performances of the first, second and third seances and after having the subject open his eyes and keep them open, suggestion may be made that will give evidence of absolute control over his five senses. It is best to make such suggestions as will gradually lead from one of the senses to the others. For example:

"The day is cold. You are shivering. Here, put on this overcoat. See, the snow is falling, listen to the sleigh bells. Here comes a sleigh. Jump in and take a ride. This is delightful. Oh, my, the sleigh has upset. You have injured your arm. It is paining you. Here is some ammonia liniment. Smell it. Look out, it is strong. Never mind, it won't burn you. Rub it on your arm. Now, the pain is stopped. Take a little of this ginger ale to warm you up. Now you feel better. Let us get in the sleigh again. All right now, here we go."

By such a train of suggestions you have influenced the senses of feeling, seeing, hearing, smelling and tasting and we have made him realize the disagreeable sensation of pain and have banished it and also excited in him the emotion of joy. Henceforth you can make him realize anything you may suggest. You have him under absolute control.

It is always best to connect the senses in harmonious relationship and not excite them individually and abruptly.

### THE FIFTH SEANCE.

The fifth seance may be given over to various experiments characteristic of the somnambulistic state; such as singing, dancing, declaiming, fascination, anaesthesia, post-suggestion, etc. Clairvoyance belongs to the somnambulistic state, but it should not be attempted until after the subject has been under your influence many times, and then it will not be successful unless the subject is especially adapted to it. See Chapter VIII.

### THE SIXTH SEANCE.

The sixth seance may be devoted to inducing the cataleptic condition. After bringing the subject into the somnambulistic state, suggest that his muscles and joints are getting so stiff that he cannot move them. Make passes down his arms and legs and press the joints as though you were tightening them and he will soon be stiff as a board. After this has once been accomplished, you can instantly produce catalepsy by sudden suggestion and the subject will remain immovable in the attitude assumed at the time of the suggestion. Release the subject from the cataleptic state by suggesting that he can now use his muscles and give him some pleasant movements to perform. Never awaken him entirely with abruptness from the cataleptic condition.

## PROOF OF HYPNOTIC ABILITY.

After you have succeeded in carrying your subject successfully through the experiments enumerated, or similar ones, you may rest assured that you can accomplish whatever any other hypnotist has accomplished. You will need practice before you can influence more than a small percentage of persons, and these must be for some time such as you are confident are not your superiors in will power, social standing or education. Repeated experiments will soon give you confidence in your ability and it will not be long before you can control eighty per cent of those whom you meet. Your confidence in your hypnotic power will counterbalance all deference to your otherwise superiors.

The lethargic condition should not be induced for purpose of amusement. There is no reason why any subject should be placed in a deathlike sleep. You can exercise such power, but it is wisest not to do so, except for purely scientific reasons and then only with the full consent of the subject.

You may be able to develop subjects in two or three seances, but the deeper degrees of hypnosis are not usually developed until the fourth or fifth. With rare exceptions, you will in six or seven seances, gain as full control over your subject as it is possible for you ever to secure, though you may do better with a different subject.

# CHAPTER XIII.

## ANIMAL MAGNETISM—MAGNETIC HEALING.

The employment of animal magnetism in the treatment of disease has constituted an important part in the general practice of a number of prominent physicians for many years. These physicians have not, as a rule, made a conspicuous display of their knowledge of the subject, realizing that the public in general were not prepared to sufficiently differentiate between their methods and those employed by ignorant charlatans. Nevertheless the great success that attended their efforts to relieve suffering through what we now call hypnotic influence, led them to impress upon their professional brethren the importance of a more thorough study of this valuable branch of medicine.

Among the first in America to employ "animal magnetism" in medical practice, was Alva Curtis, A. M., M. D., a highly educated and talented physician, who died in 1881. He attributed his remarkable success in practice to the scientific use of non-poisonous remedies and the mental influence he was able to exert over his patients. While not claiming to be a "magnetic healer," he nevertheless practiced and taught to his classes the art of "magnetizing," and as early as 1846, he published the formulated principles of animal magnetism that have ever since formed the basis of the practice of magnetic healing. The author, like many others, is greatly indebted to the genius and erudition of this remarkable teacher who devoted his life to the amelioration of his fellow men.

### PHILOSOPHY AND METHOD OF DR. CURTIS.

The brain is a compound organ, to the distinct portions of which is assigned the performance of special mental functions. These separate portions, or organs, can be readily excited by the touch of the hand, and can be made to perform not only the peculiar functions of the brain, but of those of all the other portions of the body, increasing or depressing them at pleasure.

Magnetism (neuraura) may be made to proceed at will from every organ of the brain of every person, and to affect to some extent the organs of any other brain to which the fingers of the operator may be applied. Of course, the more of this magnetism a person has, the more effectually he can operate upon others; and the less he possesses, the more distinctly he perceives the influence of those who have the most. Those who have the least magnetism are termed impressibles. So sensitive are some of these to the influence of the magnetism of others, that whenever they touch an organ of the head or face of another, they feel, in themselves, the influence of the action of that organ, as strong or weak, healthy or unhealthy, and are consequently capable of determining the relative power of different brains, or of the different organs of the same brain.

### HOW TO DETERMINE IMPRESSIBLES.

To ascertain whether or not a person is impressible, take a smooth, metallic rod, about half an inch in diameter and a foot long. Put one end of this rod into the left hand of the subject and request him to hold it loosely; while with your own hand you grasp firmly the other end for some five to thirty minutes. If he is impressible and if you are a good operator, he will feel a diminution of sensibility, or a numbness (much like that of the limb going to sleep) creeping up his wrist, arm and shoulder and perhaps into his body. Some have described it as resembling a charge of electricity when insulated. If no impression should be made, either the subject is not very impressible or you are not a good operator. But if impressible at all, his organs are not all equally so. Those organs are the most impressible which have been the most frequently and powerfully irritated and inflamed. If the irritation and inflammation have become chronic, the effect is of a depressing character and in proportion to the recovery of a healthy tone this impressibility wears away. In other words, the subject acquires more power to resist the impressions of the operators.

Every organ in the brain, as well as the body, has its anatgonistic organ, which is known through the study of phrenology. All these organs are constantly working in opposition to one another, so that a man's character is not decided by the strength or activity of either one of these, but by the balance of power between them.

The impressible subject feels very manifestly, whether pleasantly or painfully, the influence of the organ with which he is brought in contact. To prevent this influence from being disagreeable, he should always keep one hand near the antagonist of an organ when examining it with the other, so that if a disagreeable impression is about to be established, he can so touch the antagonist and restore his balance.

Having found a suitable, that is, a very impressible subject, he can determine by feeling on other heads, the locality of all those organs that are very active or much depressed, and thus ascertain the extremes of character or of disease, much better than he can their middle ground. Impressibles can operate on themselves, so as to relieve their own pains and aches.

### TO RELIEVE HEADACHE.

Ascertain where the pain is. Place yourself on the opposite side; put the points of the fingers of both your hands on the seat of the pain. Then brush quickly, but lightly, from that point toward you and outward, occasionally putting your hands on the organs antagonistic to the seat of the pain, till the head appears to be equally excited; that is, as full of blood and heat in one part as in another, when you should brush downward and outward until the effect is produced. If the forehead aches, stand behind the patient and brush backward. If the back of the head is affected, stand before him and brush forward. If the top should ache, brush downward. If one side aches, brush toward the other side. In nearly every case this will give quick relief, and if the headache is due to mental disturbance, the relief will be permanent.

### TO RELIEVE TOOTHACHE.

Brush with one hand from the point over the tooth in the direction of the nerve toward the ear, and press with the other hand pretty hard on the organs of conscientiousness, firmness, self-esteem, and approbativeness, till the effect is produced. This must be continued for five minutes to an hour, according to the impressibility of the patient and the severity of the toothache. Almost any toothache may be temporarily relieved by this method; although, of course, it will not give permanent relief if the difficulty is caused by cold or exposed nerves.

### TO RELIEVE BODILY PAINS.

Pains in any part of the body may often be removed by a similar method. With one hand brush from the seat of the pain to opposite parts of the body and at the same time place the other hand upon the restraining organs of the head—firmness, self-esteem, conscientiousness and approbativeness, among which the point between conscientiousness and cautiousness seems the most prominent. Slight pressure on this region will remove any feeling of depression in any part of the body, as sickness in the stomach, pain in the bowels, oppression of the lungs, pain about the heart, sense of suffocation, pain in the side, etc.

### TO PRODUCE SLEEP.

To produce natural sleep, place your hand upon the forehead, with the fore and second finger astride the nose; bring them up into the arch of the eye, and press very gently for some minutes. In this manner the most restless persons can be put to sleep, even those upon whom medicines and nervines have no apparent effect. Persons in the greatest mental excitement, amounting to extreme nervous tremor, may by this method in a few minutes be restored to the utmost calmness. Even spasms have been relaxed and the system restored to quietness, by brushing the action first equally in all parts of the head, and thence into and out of the body, as before directed.

### SUPPRESSION OF THE RESPIRATION.

Too rapid breathing may be restored to the normal, and natural breathing may be greatly reduced in frequency, by placing the fingers on the cheeks each side of the mouth. When the breathing is too slow, it may be hastened by gently making pressure on the restraining organs on the upper part of the back of the head. Care must always be exercised in resorting to these methods. In some cases, as in asphyxiation, the latter mentioned procedure will be found valuable.

### REGIONS OF THE BRAIN.

In general, the energies of the bodies are affected in the following manner by the various regions of the brain. They are depressed by the forehead, the face and the neck before the ears. They are strengthened and restored by the upper and back portions of the brain. They are propelled by the lower and back portions of the brain.

More particularly, the lower portion of the front of the head contains the perceptive faculties; while the intellectual faculties are contained in the upper portion of the front of the head. The central and upper portions of the head are moral and religious; the back and upper portions of the head are affective; while the lower and back portions are propelling. The bases of the back portions control the animal actions, and the bases of the front portions govern the internal organs.

Every part of the brain receives impressions from, or throws influence to, some part or portion of the body. Imagine central points in these regions radiating toward one another in exact proportions and you can conceive a well-balanced brain. Unusual relationship displays an unevenly balanced brain. Realizing the faculties controlled by the various regions it is then easy by manipulations to equalize action by passes from any region to its antagonistic region—from intellectual to animal, for instance.

### DOCTRINES OF MAGNETIC HEALING.

1. Every person is susceptible to magnetic influence, and also capable of successfully resisting a degree of it equal to his own magnetic power, and of sustaining a higher degree, so far as to be little affected by the magnetism of another.

2. Every person is capable of communicating animal magnetism to others; but if the person to whom he attempts to communicate it possesses as

high a degree of the same power as he does, no distinct manifestation of the influence will be perceived.

3. Persons possess at different times different degrees of magnetic power, and also different degrees of impressibility. Consequently the same class of experiments, by the same persons, will sometimes be successful and sometimes fail.

4. Experiments with the sick, if judiciously conducted, seldom fail to afford relief; and if disease should be entirely of a nervous character, permanent recovery will usually follow.

5. If susceptibility to animal magnetism is a quality or power of the nerves themselves, it is always improved and rendered more acute and distinct by exercise. If the susceptibility is the result of disease, it generally diminishes as the patient recovers. In other words, it requires more magnetic power to influence a healthy organ than it does to influence a diseased organ.

6. The most important faculty in an operator is his ability to concentrate his mind. For want of this ability, many who possess a high degree of animal magnetism are very poor operators, when they should be most successful. The power of concentration of mind may be greatly increased by persevering practice.

7. By judicious scientific experiments in animal magnetism, every depressed part of the body may be brought into a condition of natural activity, inde-

pendent of the action of other organs, and may be forced to perform its particular function in a natural manner without interfering with other organs. That is, it is possible to stimulate a depressed organ without over-stimulating organs that are working naturally.

8.  Through animal magnetism the seat and character of disease may be ascertained and the proper means of restoration indicated.  Also, the improvement or decline of the patient's condition may be noted from day to day.

1.  Do not operate upon persons who are seriously affected in the vital organs unless you are yourself strong and in good health; otherwise, through your own impressibility, you may receive from them the symptoms of their diseases, instead of communicating to them the beneficial influences of your own system.

2.  In treating diseased persons, if you wish to stimulate or arouse to activity any special organ that is depressed, while directing your magnetism to that organ, always keep one hand near the antagonistic organ of the patient or of a sound and healthy bystander.

### PRECAUTIONS TO BE OBSERVED.

3.  If operating upon persons who are passionate by nature or easily angered, be careful not to excite their organs of combativeness, destructiveness, etc., unless provided with assistance to control them. If by accident or design you should happen to excite

these organs, and the subject should become out-rageous, touch the organs of benevolence and rev-erence and the excitement will subside by equalizing the nervous action.

### HOW TO MAGNETIZE A PERSON.

Place the subject on a chair before you, a little lower than your own, if convenient, and in a per-fectly easy position with his feet near together. Request him to relax his whole system and to look steadily into your eyes as long as he can keep his own open, and to close his eyes when they become heavy and difficult to keep open. Enforce rigid silence upon all others who may be in the room or immediately adjacent rooms.

Seat yourself before the subject in a very easy position; your feet each side of his, and your body straight—indicating self-confidence. Put the balls of your two thumbs upon the balls of his, as they lie at ease on his lap. Turn your fingers into the palms of his hands, and communicate to them a slight mus-cular tension. Look steadily into the pupils of his eyes without winking. Make no motions of any character except those compelled by breathing, which should be steady and regular. Constantly will to yourself that he should go to sleep, and think of nothing else until his eyes close and remain so. When he is evidently asleep, let go his hands and make passes with the fingers from the crown of the head forward over the face, down over the shoulders and arms to the hands and outward, returning your hands with the palms outward, to the top of the head, whence you should proceed as before, occasionally making passes down the breast.

The passes of the hand should be light. They may not even touch the body, or they may slightly brush it and occasionally rest a few seconds on the shoulders, breast or stomach, until the subject is in a deep sleep. This may be known by the action of his hands, which will be attracted to your own as a needle to a magnet; or by the fact, as a rule, that he will not answer any questions put to him by any other person than the operator. Some subjects will sleep, although not very profoundly, and not exhibit these signs. In general, the subject becomes rigid in his limbs, but to this rule there are many exceptions. When very rigid, the tension should be relieved by reverse passes.

### EXPERIMENTS IN ANIMAL MAGNETISM.

When your subject is asleep, you may take into your mouth anything that has a peculiar taste, and he will taste as you taste; and if he is familiar with the article, he will give you its name when he awakens. Cleanse your mouth thoroughly, and taste of something else, and he will feel and act as before, as long as you have yourself a distinct perception of the article. In these experiments the mildest and most volatile articles should be chosen first, as a powerful and permanent stimulant taken first will remain with those taken later and confuse the impressions they may make.

If you inflict pain upon yourself in any way, the subject will feel and describe it. If you should be gloomy or happy, irritated or calm, your subject will be likewise. If you are diseased, you ought not to magnetize anyone, it will injure you as well as the subject; not seriously, but unpleasantly. If you cannot at all times, under the most provoking circumstances, keep your own temper and retain an even balance of all your feelings, you are not a proper person to experiment with the influence of animal magnetism upon others. First cultivate the power of self-control and then practice magnetism upon others.

### TO EXAMINE DISEASED PERSONS.

In order to diagnose disease through the influence of animal magnetism, three persons must be present at the sitting, namely, the operator, the subject and the patient. It is the duty of the operator to place the subject in a deep sleep, by the methods given and to then make magnetic connection between the sleeping subject and the patient.

After the subject has been thoroughly placed under the influence of animal magnetism, have the patient take a seat beside him and then join their hands. Gently, by passes with the hands, brush from the sleeping subject the "magnetism" into the patient, in the manner of making these passes as above described, and continue doing so until the subject will answer freely any questions put to him by the patient concerning his condition of health. If the subject should be asked by the patient: "What is the matter with me?" the reply would not be directly: "You have a cancer," or whatever might be the difficulty. He will avoid direct answers and perhaps pause or refuse to reply until led on by indirect questions, such as: "How are my lungs, my stomach, my liver, kidneys, etc.?" naming the various organs and structures slowly, giving him time to reply to each. To such questions he will reply: "This organ is inflamed." "That is inactive." "This is ulcerated." "That is hardened." "This is improving." "That is growing worse." In many instances, if the sleeping subject should be familiar with medicines, he will advise the use of certain remedies of a harmless nature. It seems remarkable that the diagnosis made by subjects through magnetism is usually correct and often arrived at very quickly, although physicians had previously attempted in vain to arrive at a satisfactory conclusion.

Through the general use of animal magnetism, where the physician is the operator and the patient is the subject, much good can be accomplished. In nervous disturbances it is especially valuable. Hysterical persons are much relieved and quieted by suitable passes; wakefulness is overcome and refreshing sleep is secured, and delirium often speedily and effectually subdued, much more readily than by the use of medicines. In the course of fevers, this method of quieting restlessness is extremely valuable and highly appreciated by the patient and members of the household.

In most cases it would be unwise for a physician to make any special display or utter any claims concerning his magnetic powers. He might at once be classed as "a fake magnetic healer," etc. But by exercising good judgment he can so use his powers as to cause the friends to exclaim: "Why, doctor, you must have some magnetic influence over your patient, for you no sooner come near him than he seems better." His very presence can, by magnetic influence he exerts, become a valuable aid in the cure of disease, and his power will be a means of securing from his patients that implicit confidence which is so necessary for the successful practice of medicine.

# CHAPTER XIV.

## OVERCOMING HABITS BY HYPNOTISM.

Nature of habits—Drugs of no avail—Suggestion the basis of
sanitarium treatment—Morphine and alcohol cures—How
hypnotism overcomes habits—Currents of nerve force—
Memory and post-hypnotism—Frightened horses—Tobacco
habit cured—Cause and cure of stammering—Cigarette
smoking—Cure of other habits.

A habit is the mental inability to prevent the frequent repetition of an action. Persons who suffer
from bad habits would, as a rule, gladly overcome
them if they could, but they cannot do so without
help. Punishment will not help them, for that only
increases their mental inability by forcing upon them
the consciousness of their weakness. When anyone
addicted to a habit becomes convinced of his ability
to overcome it, half the battle is won, although when
his efforts are followed by failure his self-confidence
soon vanishes.

Medicines are of no avail in curing habits. It is
true that most excellent results have occasionally
been obtained in the treatment of the opium habit,
the liquor habit, etc., but the careful investigation of
those cases would show that the patients were
usually under rigid control for weeks or months;

that they were given no opportunity to repeat their injurious actions and that the medicines used were employed for correcting the abnormal conditions resulting from the bad habits and not for the purpose of "curing the mind."

In some methods of treating bad habits, strychnia and other nerve destroyers are used for the direct purpose of destroying functional activity of the nervous system. They make wrecks of the mind and body and cannot be called cures.

Again, many persons addicted to the morphine or liquor habits voluntarily place themselves in sanitariums or retreats, widely advertised as places where these habits are positively cured. It is a fact that many are benefited by going to such institutions, but the real benefit obtained is due to the suggestions impressed upon the mind. Everything suggests to the patient a cure of his habit. The advertisements he read positively asserted that he could be cured, the letters he received from the institution told him in emphatic terms that all he had to do was to "come and be cured;" he went and the doctors and the nurses impressed upon him that a cure was certain and he became convinced, and under their influence he restrained his habit and became confident, and if he was cured it was the result of forcible action upon his mind. In fact, it was a cumbersome, protracted and expensive method of overcoming his habit which might have been easily and quickly cured by hypnotism. In these sanitariums, outside of the treatment of the body, given to overcome the effects of the bad habits, the only actual benefit given the patient in his mental efforts, is the suggestion or semi-hypnotism forced upon him. Direct hypnotism is far more effective and it is encouraging to know that the medical profession is gradually realizing its power in these cases. The future is full of promise to those willing to avail themselves of the advantages of this marvelous science.

How does hypnotism overcome a habit? To answer the question scientifically would require the use of much technical language, to understand which would necessitate a complete knowledge of the physiology of the brain and nervous system. But as this work was not compiled for the exclusive use of physicians and scientists, a simple answer to the question can be given in figurative language.

Our voluntary actions are controlled by our thoughts, and our thoughts can be likened to "currents" of nerve force, making impressions upon brain tissues. When these currents repeatedly flow in the same manner upon the same tissues, lasting impressions are made, and the actions they prompt become almost involuntary. During the state of hypnosis the mind is absolutely passive and the operator can direct the subject's current of thought in any manner he may choose. By sudden and forcible suggestion he can turn the current abruptly out of its well-worn channel, and by repetitions of this forcible suggestion he is enabled to cause the current of thought to permanently abandon its old groove and allow the traces of its deep impressions upon the brain tissues to become obliterated. This explanation must not be taken literally, but it serves to convey the idea of how hypnotic influence overcomes bad habits.

A great many intricate theories have been offered in explanation of memory and its association with objects. The figurative statements just made help us to fix in our own minds the nature of this association and will enable us to better understand the process of post-hypnotism, which is the essential act in curing bad habits.

While the subject is in the hypnotic state and his mind passive, impressions are easily made. At that time let the operator associate the idea of tobacco, for instance, with the thought of abhorrence, and let this be often repeated; then ever afterward, almost unconsciously, the idea of tobacco will arouse abhorrence, and this can be overcome only as other habits can be overcome.

A well known illustration of this line of associating ideas of objects with emotions, may be appropriately mentioned. Let a horse become thoroughly frightened at an object, for instance suppose he should step through a broken plank on a certain bridge, then ever afterward he would become frightened when crossing that bridge, and shy to one side, even though the old plank were replaced by a new one. Upon his passive mind a vivid impression had been made, and the idea of the object caused the current of thought to flow in that deep groove. Only constant effort or some counteracting influence can disassociate the idea of the object and the thought of fear.

### CURED THE TOBACCO HABIT.

A gentleman from Iowa, Mr. John T. Boyer, a few years ago called upon me for the medical treatment of his wife, which necessitated their remaining in the city for several weeks. He was an inveterate chewer of tobacco and expressed the most ardent desire to overcome the habit. He had made many vain attempts to do so and had fruitlessly used various anti-tobacco preparations. In the course of a conversation with him upon the subject of hypnotism I made the emphatic assertion that through the hypnotic method I could completely cure him of his habit before his wife should be able to return home. He agreed to remain with her and submit to my hypnotic influence.

For some reason Mr. Boyer was hard to hypnotize, my first and second attempts exhausted me without inducing hypnosis in him, but the third attempt was successful. After first getting him into the profound stage, I gave him a piece of plug tobacco to chew, informing him that it was a special brand from Cuba. He relished it immensely. Soon I informed him that, although it was such a superior tobacco it possessed the peculiarity that he could not get it out of his mouth. This startled him for awhile and then with a broad grin on his face he chewed furiously. In a short time I said:

"Well, you can't get that out of your mouth, that's certain, and you can't stop chewing it; but you've made an awful mistake—the tobacco is nothing but cat filth."

The scene that followed was ludicrous. He contorted his face frightfully, turned up his nose, gagged himself, twisted his body, walked back and forth, threw himself on the floor, and finally reached a state of agony, when I suddenly exclaimed:

"Now you can stop chewing; now you can spit it out of your mouth. Here, wash out your mouth with this water."

He lost no time, and eagerly cleansed his mouth with the imaginary water which I pretended to hand to him in a glass. After he had quieted down I emphatically stated, in slow, monotonous tones:

"Every piece of tobacco that you may try to chew will have cat filth in it. It will make you deathly sick; leave it alone."

Then, by the customary method, I awakened him. The next time I placed him under the influence I offered him imaginary chewing gum, and then told him that he could not stop chewing and that it was tobacco and not chewing gum, and finally that the tobacco contained cat filth. This plan I adopted in all my work upon him. Altogether, I hypnotized him twelve times in four weeks. Before he left the city he was entirely cured of the tobacco habit, although he had no recollection of his experience while in the hypnotic state. It was very gratifying, as well as amusing, to watch him when offered a piece of tobacco. He would look at it in such a peculiarly suspicious manner and sniff its odor with evident disgust, and then hand it back with the remark:

"I really don't care for it; it seems to me it would make me sick if I should try to chew it."

Mr. Boyer's aversion to tobacco has remained with him ever since, and my success in his case has aided me in overcoming the habit in others.

### AS A CURE FOR STUTTERING.

When deformities of the organs of speech cause stuttering, hypnotism cannot be utilized as a means of cure; but when stuttering is due to habit or nervous conditions, then hypnotism can confidently be relied upon, and is probably the only effective method that gives prompt results. In most cases two or three weeks' time, embracing ten or twelve sittings, will be sufficient. My method of curing stuttering through hypnotism is well illustrated by the case of Daniel McIntyre, a young man nineteen years old, who had stuttered ever since he was six years old. The habit was most likely formed by a severe scolding and whipping given to him at that time by his father for some trivial offense. It took most persistent inquiry to ascertain this fact; but it is always important to realize the origin of the habit, for such knowledge may be an aid in effecting a cure.

Young McIntyre had followed the usual course

of those endeavoring to break the habit, but every method he tried brought forcibly upon him the consciousness of his habit. My hypnotic method did exactly the reverse. After getting him completely under control, he was made to believe that a valuable prize had been offered to the person who could repeat most rapidly the well-known word tests:

"Peter Piper picked a peck of pickled peppers; a peck of pickled peppers Peter Piper picked. If Peter Piper picked a peck of pickled peppers, where's the peck of pickled peppers Peter Piper picked?"

"Theophilus thrust three thousand thistles through the thick of his thumb. If Theophilus thrust three thousand thistles through the thick of his thumb, where are the three thousand thistles that Theophilus thrust through the thick of his thumb?"

"Now, Daniel," I said, "these are the hardest sentences anyone can pronounce, and very few people can pronounce them rapidly; but you can, and you must practice and see how fast you can repeat them."

At each sitting he would repeat these tests twenty or thirty times, always accurately. Finally he was made to believe that the examination was taking place, and then that he won the prize. And it was impressed upon him time and again that he was a fluent speaker and able to repeat rapidly all the most difficult tests. It was most interesting to watch his expression of delight and of self-approbation during these sittings. During the first two weeks, when not under hypnotic control, he seemed to stutter worse than ever, but during the third week improvement was rapid, and after the sitting in which he won the prize he had no further trouble.

Self-consciousness while speaking is the most common cause of stuttering, and stutterers cannot shake off the feeling that others are criticising their language. There comes to my mind the recollection of a married man who was never known to speak correctly until he was once overheard talking glibly and correctly to his infant child when he thought no one else was near. He knew the child could not criticise his language, and lost his self-consciousness.

Probably no bad habit is easier to overcome by hypnotism than the habit of cigarette smoking, which has become widespread and fraught with great danger to both mind and body. The subjects are usually hypnotized very easily, and readily obey post-hypnotic suggestions. In these cases one precaution must be observed: Do not place the subject in the lethargic or cataleptic starte. The heart is usually too weak to permit this condition with safety. In general, the breaking of the cigarette habit by hypnotism is essentially the same as the method adopted for the cure of the tobacco habit.

Various other bad habits could be mentioned that have been quickly overcome, and any one who has mastered the art of hypnotism can accomplish great good in this line of work. If the science were valuable for no other purpose, its study should be encouraged. But when we realize the multitude of other benefits to be derived froom hypnotism, we cannot but regard it as one of the greatest of all the branches of science, and the future opens a marvelous field of usefulness to those who intelligently study its philosophy and practical application.

# CHAPTER XV.

## CRIMINAL HYPNOTISM.

Hypnotism does not corrupt morals—Sensational newpaper
articles—Stole while hypnotized—Melancholy induced by
a discarded suitor—Elopement due to hypnotic influence—
Sensational reports—Trained criminals—Hypnotism an
excuse—A drug clerk's error—Possibilities of crime—Possibility of bodily harm—Confidence in the operator.

The claim that hypnotism is frequently used to
produce criminals and to aid in the perpetuation of
crime is based more upon the imagination than upon
fact. It can no more corrupt the moral senses of
those subjected to its influences than it can instill
conscience, morality, and integrity into the human
character.

The term "Criminal Hypnotism" is on a par with
such evident misnomers as criminal astronomy, criminal chemistry, criminal mechanics, etc. These
sciences do not produce the desire to commit crime,
although they impart knowledge that an evil-minded
person might readily use for such purposes. For
instance, an astrologist who actually possessed an
accurate knowledge of astronomy might so impress
a credulous person as to make him believe that the
relationship of the various planets to his life made

it his inevitable destiny to commit a certain crime
Again, the knowledge of combining chemicals for
the manufacture of dynamite and other dangerous
explosives, or the preparation of deadly potions,
might suggest their criminal use. But it is certain
that unless there pre-existed a criminal tendency,
these sciences would not create it, and to discourage
their study on account of criminal possibilities would
be exceedinly narrow minded.

It can be positively asserted that a virtuous subject cannot be demoralized by ordinary hypnotic
control. Suggestions repugnant to the subject's
innate sense of morality and uprightness will either
produce instant awakening or result in emphatic
disobedience. The disposition of the subject cannot
be altered by hypnosis.

Contrary to these facts are many sensational newspaper articles upon the relation of hynotism to crime.
It seems to have been a favorite topic for the furtive
brain and ready pen of the ordinary newspaper writer,
who is anxious to satisfy the public craving for
morbid exaggerations, rather than desirous of fur-
nishing reliable information. The following clippings
from daily newspapers are good examples of the
perverted ideas of hypnotism conveyed to the public
by these sensational newspaper writers:

### STOLE WHILE HYPNOTIZED.

"A peculiar case came up in Justice Pelham's Court
yesterday. Otto Fischer, a young man twenty-five
years old, was arraigned upon the charge of burg-

lary. He was arrested Thursday night by Officer Maloney as he was leaving the rear door of Burton & Hooker's dry goods store, 263 West Third Street, carrying with him several bolts of silk dress goods. His novel defense was the statement that he had been for two days under the control of a hypnotist, who had paid him a dollar a day for the privilege of experimenting upon him. He said he had called upon the hypnotist two hours before he was arrested and had allowed himself to be hypnotized, after which he could recollect nothing until awakened by the shock of arrest. He could not give the name or address of the hypnotist who had induced him to commit the crime. His case was given a continuance until next Thursday, in order to afford him an opportunity to recall the events and places that could enable him to prove his claim of innocence and fix the guilt upon the party who hypnotized him."

### REMARKABLE HYPNOTIC POWER.

"Minnie Teufel, aged nineteen, was yesterday sent to the insane asylum, suffering from profound melancholia, induced by the hypnotic power of a former suitor whom she had rejected. She has been in this condition for six weeks. It was brought upon her suddenly as she passed the unscrupulous hypnotist in the street. She left her home in the best of spirits and returned in the sad condition which now ruins her life. The hypnotist left the city after performing his evil work, and friends of the girl threaten dire vengeance upon him when he returns, unless he is able to restore Miss Teufel to her right mind."

## HOME WRECKED BY HYPNOTISM.

"A sad case of the evil influence that can be exerted by an unscrupulous hypnotist has lately startled the aristocratic suburb of Clifton, and while it serves well to illustrate the danger to society made possible by this latest fad, it also serves to explain many incidents that have led to the condemnation instead of the pity of its victims. About a month ago Clifton society missed the presence of one of its most popular leaders, whose name is withheld for obvious reasons. It was reported that she was visiting relatives in the east and would shortly return. Her husband, a prominent business man, and her relatives were the only ones who knew her absence to be due to her elopement with a well-known attorney. Her return the latter part of the week was brought about by her realization of the terrible mistake she had made and remorse for her act. It seems that the young attorney who wrought such havoc in her home had much leisure time on his hands, and employed it in studying the occult sciences, among which was the art of hypnotism, which he readily mastered. Not content to practice it upon subjects hired for the purpose, he endeavored to bring his friends under his influence, and succeeded so remarkably well that he was soon making boasts of his power over the numerous ladies who favored him with the hospitality of their homes. The prominence and popularity of the parties concerned forbid the statement of particulars, but enough has been said to explain the fascination that led a wife and mother to desert husband and children and wreck her home and bring disgrace upon herself and family. That such havoc can be wrought by hypnotism, even in a single instance, demonstrates the dangers run by those who are introducing it into society as a fad and a means of amusement."

The columns of a daily newspaper necessarily contain much that is written by incompetent persons, but the influence of its articles is great. Such articles as are quoted above have had much to do in causing great misunderstanding concerning the powers and uses of hypnotism. It cannot be properly judged by the statements of those incompetent to explain its powers, and the rash and sensational statements of newspaper reporters should be taken for what they are worth, and not be given credit for scientific accuracy. The average reporter is no more competent to explain the subject of hypnotism than he is to explain the other branches of science.

It is, of course, possible, for a designing person, skilled in the art of hypnotism, to induced trained subjects to commit crimes for which they should not be held altogether accountable, but such instances are extremely rare, and are always associated with facts that explain them. It is no argument against hypnotism to assert or even to prove that it can be advantageously used for criminal purposes. The same arguments would apply equally well against the use of chloroform and other anaesthetics. These agents are constantly being employed for criminal purposes, and can exert their influences upon every one, while comparatively few can be hypnotized without repeated trials, and many not at all.

It requires absolute hypnotic control over a person to induce him to commit an act that is at entire variance with his wishes and sense of propriety or honor. This fact renders absurd the frequent pleas made by persons accused of a crime that they were under the influence of some one who must have hypnotized them. A drug clerk declared that a customer hypnotized him into selling a deadly poison which was used for criminal purposes. He claimed that he actually thought he was dispensing an innocent agent. Another drug clerk tried to excuse his dispensing of alcoholic liquors at retail by the statement that the parties to whom he sold it had for some time exercised a hypnotic control over him. Not infrequently persons guilty of larceny, assault and other misdemeanors are quick to lay the blame upon the hypnotic influence of others over them. It is safe to say that not in one instance out of ten thousands of these claims is there any foundation for them. Those who make them have heard or read the sensational side of hypnotism and are ready to shield themselves behind its mysteries. It is strange that any attention whatever is paid to their claims, and there probably would not be were it not for the general clamor for the sensational in any form.

While it is true that there is no such thing as criminal hypnotism, yet it is necessary to realize the possibilities of crime in connection with the practice of this art. A base and criminal nature always seeks means of satisfying itself, and a person desirous of doing wrong will endeavor to learn methods that will aid him in so doing. All arts and sciences can be used for base purposes, and every innocent amusement can be utilized as a game of chance; yet the arts and sciences and popular amusements are encouraged everywhere. Knowledge cannot of itself debase anyone, but a mind already debased may use knowledge to the injury of others. The science of hypnotism is no exception to the rule, and the few who use it for disreputable purposes cannot detract from its great value to mankind in general. The more it is understood, the greater will become the benefits to be derived from it.

It is possible for a hypnotist to so completely gain control over his subject as to compel obedience to his demands of a criminal nature, or to cause submission to bodily harm. But we are constantly placing our lives into the hands of others and relying upon their integrity for personal safety. The physician could easily cause the death of his patient without suspicion, the nurse could destroy the life of her charge, and in innumerable other cases crimes could be committed by those with whom we associate. It is our confidence in their integrity that causes us to think of no evil, although the opportunities for doing harm are ever present. In connection with hypnotism such opportunities are very infrequent, and need never occur.

Until the practice of hypnotism becomes more general and assumes its place among methods commonly employed for various purposes, it is advisable for the hypnotist to constantly guard against the possibility of false accusations. A third party should always be present and a subject should never be hypnotized without his personal consent or the consent of his friends. Never make a mystery of hypnotism and always let your relationship with the subject be above suspicion.

# CHAPTER XVI.

## HYPNOTISM AND DISEASE.

Influence of mind over health—Resisting contagious diseases—
Immunity of nurses—Concentration of thought—Dispensa-
tions of Providence—Protection a natural law—Mental determination—Case of Dr. Tanner—Maintenance of health
—No time to get sick—Danger in retiring from business—
Imagination and disease—Fear often causes disease—Imaginary hydrophobia—Idleness invites disease—Hypochondria—Appliances to ward off disease—Belts and charms—
Electric belts — Pilgrimages — Miracles performed at
shrines.

The greatest possible benefits to be derived from
hypnotism are those in connection with disease. The
mind exerts a wonderful influence over the health
of the body, and persons subjected to the most debil-
itating influences, and surrounded by the most unhy-
gienic conditions, have been able to ward off disease
by mental effort.

There is no preventive against contagion so effective as an absolute sense of security. It is often
asked, "Why do not physicians contract contagious
diseases from their patients?" Occasionally they
do, but as a rule their familiarity with disease gives

them a feeling of immunity, and their interest in the case and their sense of responsibility serve to engender that feeling. How frequently we hear of a wife nursing a husband through an attack of small-pox without herself contracting the disease. Ask her if she wasn't afraid of "catching it," and she will say she never thought of such a thing. Her interest lay in the patient, her mind was constantly upon his welfare, she was too unselfish to think of her own danger, and consequently she was saved from contracting the disease.

Nurses in hospitals constantly run risks of contagion, but seldom succumb. During cholera epidemics some of the most heroic deeds were performed by those who risked health and life for the benefit of others. But that heroism was their protection. In olden days the immunity of such persons from contagion was ascribed to miraculous power, and they were said to have been spared as a divine reward for their self-sacrifice. It was this belief that prompted many to offer their services during visitations of the various plagues.

In the light of modern science we realize that concentration of thought away from the idea of personal danger was the chief cause of immunity. Its explanation comes under the domain of hypnotism, and not under a special dispensation of Providence.

Is it not narrowing the actions of the Almighty down to a small personal compass to regard every individual case of protection as the result of spe-

cial decree of Providence? How much grander
appears the supreme wisdom of the Almighty when
we realize that it is a natural law that has been
obeyed, and that a natural consequence has followed. Through the study of hypnotism we are
enabled to get an insight into these laws and to
place ourselves under their control.

Virtue brings its own reward as a natural consequence. Being unselfish, and thinking not of our
own selves while striving to benefit others, will give
us immunities from many things otherwise deemed
inevitable. Missionaries have labored for years in
the leper colonies without contracting the loath-
some disease, their minds being wholly occupied in
relieving the sufferings of others. "Keep up cour-
age" is the watchword that has sustained many foot-
worn travelers and explorers through the direst
extremities.

The mental determination and resolution to attain
notoriety preserved Dr. Tanner during his famous
fast of forty days and nights—a fast unequaled by
mortal man and utterly impossible under any circumstances other than mental enthusiasm. Let a
man be forced against his will to abstain from food
for half that length of time, and he could not survive.

The maintenance of health by mental determination is within the powers of all who have ordinary
physical attainments. The resolution not to be sick
has saved many persons from attacks of disease.
The cultivation of this species of self-hypnotism can-

not be too strongly urged upon those who would live long and be successful in life.

"I haven't time to get sick," is an expression often used by business men who are straining every nerve and employing every moment in the pursuit of wealth. They speak truthfully, for they have no time to give to worrying about the risks to health they are constantly incurring.

Their friends speak of them as being "held up by the excitement." That is true. Let these same men retire from business, and see how quickly they become the prey of disease. It is a common thing to notice that when a man has amassed a fortune and retired with the intention of doing nothing but live upon its income, he soon dies, when, as his friends remark, he was just getting ready to live. The fact is, the excitement of life being over, there was no longer anything to hinder the natural consequence of the excessive strains he had endured for years.

A man long accustomed to active business cannot safely retire suddenly. He will live longer if he determines to "die in the harness." We often wonder why men of wealth keep plodding on in their old age. It seems to be an intuitive sense of safety that prompts them to do so; or, as they express it, "I long ago got into the habit of working, and I am now too old to break the habit."

Imagination exerts a powerful influence over our lives, and this is especially true in regard to the matter of disease. We are constantly witnessing evidences of this fact as manifested by our friends and acquaintances, and possibly ourselves. Fake medical men take advantage of the well-known tendency of all to imagine the worst in regard to their weaknesses and indispositions. Advertisements are prepared with sypmtoms of fatal diseases arranged in a manner calculated to make the reader believe they "fit his case exactly," and as a rule they accomplish the purpose for which they are written. They act upon the principle of suggestion made upon a mind already concentrated upon the one idea of possible sickness beyond recovery.

Possessors of family medical guides and new students of medicine, after reading and studying the symptoms of various diseases, are very apt to become convinced that some of the fatal forms of disease have a hold upon them.

During an epidemic nervous persons who dread the prevalent malady are prone to believe every indisposition a sign of the dreaded disease. They make themselves familiar with the leading symptoms and daily and hourly watch for them, and in this manner make themselves far more liable to contract the disease they so much dread. Such persons can be greatly relieved by the positive and emphatic assurance that their fears are unfounded.

A gentleman of wealth and education became convinced that he was a victim of smallpox. He had a chill, followed by a high fever, with bones aching and severe pains in the head and back.

"See," he said, "I have all the symptoms of small-pox, except the eruption, which is due to-morrow."

"Not all the symptoms," said his physician; "your tongue is clear, and that would be impossible in a case of smallpox."

The positive assertion from one who should know what he was talking about soon convinced the patient that he had a bad cold and nothing more.

A few years ago a case of unusual interest occurred in this connection. It was during the "dog days" that a crowd of boys was watching the "dog catcher" pass by with his cart. One of them conceived the idea that it would be great sport to catch one of the little boys and put him into the cart, which was empty. Accordingly a little chap was caught and thrown into the cart. The driver entered into the fun and carried the boy a couple of blocks, with his companions following. Suddenly the boy began to scream, and then to growl and to bite. This he did so violently that the cart was stopped and the boy set free. He began to snap at the others, who became alarmed and fled. The little fellow found his way home, where he terrified the family by his antics. They thought at once that he had hydro-phobia, and sent for a physician. His companions told the story of how it happened, and the facts caused a great sensation. The physician soon became convinced that the difficulty was entirely caused by

fright and the mental association of the idea of
hydrophobia with the "dog cart." The boy rolled
upon the floor and suffered frequent spasms. He
frothed at the mouth and refused to drink. After
watching him for sime time the physician said, "It
does not look like hydrophobia, for persons bitten
by mad dogs roll first on one side and then on the
other." Instantly the boy rolled from side to side.
It was then remarked that persons who had hydrophobia would always bark three times and then
growl. This the boy quickly did. Again it was
stated that mad dogs had periods of rest, during
which they would sleep soundly and snore loudly.
At once the boy shut his eyes and began to snore.
Many other suggestions were made and quickly
acted upon, until finally the matter became laughable instead of alarming, and then tiresome, when
the doctor said, "Come, Eddie, you have done
enough of this nonsense; you are all right, and
nothing is the matter with you." He rubbed his
eyes and looked strangely about him, and said, "Oh,
my! how glad I am it wasn't true," and that was the
end of his attack of hydrophobia. By the surroundings and what they suggested, and by the fright
his being thrown into the wagon caused him, the
boy had been hypnotized and acted upon suggestions until he had been forcibly awakened from the
condition of hynosis.

Incidents are not lacking where suggestions have
caused actual disease. The idle mind is most fre-

quently affected in this manner, resulting in hypochondria, which is quite frequent among the wealthy,
who have little to employ them, and seldom met
with in those who are well occupied.

Persons who are subject to hypochondria are
actual sufferers, and do in reality feels the pains
and inconveniences of which they complain. Concentration of thought upon their bodily condition
has hypnotized them, and it takes but the merest
suggestion of a pain or of disease to affect them,
which suggestion may come through reading symptoms or by a casual remark of a friend, or by seeing
or hearing of others suffering.

# CHAPTER XVII.

## ANAESTHESIA DURING HYPNOSIS.

Freedom from pain through hypnosis—Religious ecstasy—
Queen Jezebel's priests—Ghost dances—Oriental devotees
—Burning of martyrs—Catalepsy produced by savage rites
—Religious fervor subduing pain—Modern instances—
Production of anaesthesia a natural endowment—How to
produce anaesthesia—Case of Robert McGann—Performance of dangerous surgical operations during hypnosis—
Minor surgical operations—Dangers of chloroform—Indiscriminate use of anaesthetics—Value of hypnotism in
surgery—Sewing the lips together—Passing pins and
needles through the cheek—Tongues sewed together—Dangers.

Absolute freedom from pain can be temporarily
obtained through hypnosis, and various parts of the
body can be rendered insensible to all feeling. This
fact is one of the most valuable attributes of hypnotism, and is destined to occupy an important part
in the surgery of the future.

For centuries the phenomenon of anaesthesia
under mental influence has been observed, without
being scientifically explained. The ecstacy of religion has often played an important part in such
manifestations. On Mt. Carmel the priests of

Queen Jezebel inflicted upon their bodies mutilations of a horrible nature without apparent suffering. In America to-day the red men, during their ghost dances, thrust knives into their bodies and otherwise mutilate themselves, under the influence of frenzy, and seemingly experience no pain while doing so. This they are enabled to do by first monotonously chanting and dancing and undergoing hypnotization. Throughout India and the Orient the priests and devotees of different sects complacently undergo abuses that would be excruciating agony to others. How do they do it? Always by first rendering themselves insensible to pain by various mental influences, such as are now scientifically classed under hypnotism.

Was it not largely the religious ecstacy, associated with the frenzy of the multitude or the intensity of hatred of their persecutors and the luridness of the flames, that anaesthetized the martyrs of ancient lays while they were being burned at the stake?

Among the religious rites of many savage tribes it is customary for the priests to "sing-song" with their voices and to dance round and round, performing wonderful gyrations, until they fall insensible to the ground in the condition known as catalepsy.

Modern and civilized religions are not without their hypnotic manifestations, and religious fervor causes many of the most cultured and refined to withstand experiences they could not otherwise endure.  Notice the patience and weakness of many invalids who prize their religion above life.  Such instances are common.

It is not disrespectful or irreverent to account for such manifestations by the philosophy of hypnotism.  Religious fervor is the over-stimulation of certain brain centers, resulting in the depression of other centers.  It makes no difference whether the individual is heathen or Christian or pagan or savage, the mental causes are the same in character, and the physical results are consequently identical.

The production of anaesthesia or insensibility to physical suffering by mental influence is a wonderful power bestowed upon mankind.  It is a natural power, never fully recognized until hypnotism became a scientific study.  Now we realize that all are endowed with it, and that all can take advantage of its benefits for the good of themselves and others.

### HOW TO PRODUCE ANAESTHESIA.

Whenever it becomes desirable to produce insensibility to pain by mental influence, first place the subject in the somnambulistic state by any one of the various methods, and then gradually suggest to him that the portion of the body in which you desire anaesthesia is losing its power of sensation.  For instance, make some such suggestions as the following:

"Your arm is getting somewhat numb.  Touch it with your other hand and see if you can feel anything. No, you can't tell that it is being touched. Now pinch it. See, you don't feel anything. Here, strike it hard with this stick, and you will not feel it. Why, you can do whatever you want with it, and you will not feel the pain. It is absolutely insensible to all pain."

The following case in practice illustrates the ordinary method of procedure:

Robert McGann, a woodworker, twenty-six years of age, presented himself at the clinic with a badly mutilated thumb. It had been crushed in the cogwheels of a machine and was manifestly beyond all hope of being saved. He realized that it must be removed, but was loud in his protestations against "taking chloroform."

Here was a case where hypnotism was clearly indicated, and was consequently employed, with most satisfactory results. The patient was ignorant of what hypnotism meant and had not even heard of it. He was approached in the following manner:

"Well, you plainly see that we will have to cut off your thumb. But you say you will not take chloroform, so we will have to use another method, because you can't stand the pain of an operation."

"But I'll not take cocaine, either. My brother-in-law's cousin took it at the dentist's to get a tooth pulled out, and they had to work with him for five hours to save his life."

"No, we'll not give you cocaine, either; we'll hypnotize you, and then cut it off."

"Hypnertize me! Sure, what's that?"

"Well, that means that we will all keep very quiet and let you go to sleep, and when you are sound asleep we will cut off the thumb without your knowing it, and you will not feel a particle of pain."

"Ah, I see; you mean to give me morphine or opium and make me sleep. But I'll not take a bit of it. My wife's Uncle Jerry took some of it once to stop the pain of the rheumatism, and he forgot to wake up again. No, sir; I'm not going to be killed because I got my thumb smashed. None of your poisons for me."

Then it was explained to him, in as plain language as possible, just what hypnotism really meant. He listened with the greatest attention, and the idea pleased him wonderfully.

"That's the business," he said. "Go ahead; I'm ready. Put me to sleep and swack the old thumb off of me as soon as you can."

He was put to sleep by the ordinary method, and when in profound hypnosis the following appropriate suggestions were made to him:

"Robert, you have hurt your thumb; look at it carefully, and the more you look at it the less it will pain you. Watch it very closely. The pain is leaving; it doesn't pain you at all."

His countenance assumed a look of intense interest and his eyes became riveted upon the unfortunate member. When the pain apparently vanished a happy smile spread over his face. A few passes were then made over his forehead and downward over the body, and with great emphasis, and very slowly, he was spoken to as follows:

"Your arm is getting stiff; it is very stiff; you can't move it, but it doesn't hurt you in the least. Your thumb is no good to you and you want it cut off. Sit perfectly still. We will cut off your thumb and do it without hurting you at all. You will like to watch us do it."

By such words he was kept perfectly motionless during the whole operation, which was quickly performed, without its giving him the least twinge of pain. He was a most interested spectator and smiled pleasantly at all movements, being desirous that the operation should be performed. The stitches were inserted and the stump carefully dressed before he was gradually aroused.

"Now everything is finished; you can move your arms, and there is no pain. There will be no pain. You are glad the thumb is off. Wake up! Wake up!"

He woke up, and from that moment Robert McGann became an earnest advocate of hypnotism. His case was one of many others equally successful. This kind of work can be done for nearly all patients requiring minor surgical operations.

A few cases of the performance of dangerous surgical operations under the influence of hypnosis have been recorded. That more have not been performed in this manner is probably due to the fact that but few surgeons who perform capital opera⸱ tions are hypnotists, and those few are unable to persuade their patients to submit to this method. When a subject cannot fully believe that he can be hypnotized sufficiently to safely undergo a danger- ous operation while under the influence of hypnotism, it is best not to undertake it, for the surgeon would be liable to great damage were an accident to happen under such circumstances. At the present time the benefits and powers of hypnotism are not sufficiently well known by the public to make it possible to find many who would give their consent.

In the peformance of minor surgical operations it is different. In such cases persons are always anxious to avoid taking chloroform or ether, and can be readily persuaded to allow the operation to be performed under hypnotic influence. Accidents do not occur and there is no liability of poor results being blamed upon the employment of hypnosis.

Probably no field promises such a wide usefulness for hypnotism at the present time as minor surgery. It will be a great blessing to humanity when all surgeons become expert hypnotists. Prof. William Young, a noted surgeon, once remarked: "When you administer chloroform to a man you shake him over his own grave." Ether is not such a danger- ous article as chloroform, but its indiscriminate use is most reprehensible.

It is true that comparatively few actually die from the effects of chloroform or ether while upon the operating table, and the introduction of these anaesthetics was a blessing to humanity. They have rendered possible the marvelous advances in surgery that have marked the last few decades. Nevertheless, there is a marked tendency to resort to their employment upon the most trivial occasions and under adverse circumstances when there is really no necessity for their use. When absolutely harmless means can be adopted to accomplish a desired result, it is manifestly wrong to employ means that place life in peril.

The value of hypnotism in surgery has been abundantly tested and absolutely proven, and some of the most advanced surgeons of the land are setting a worthy example to all others by taking advantage of its marvelous powers upon every possible occasion.

At times it is desirable, during public or private exhibitions of the powers of hypnotism, to demonstrate the possibility of producing profound anaesthesia or insensibility to pain. It is commonly done by sewing the lips together by needle and thread, or by passing hat pins through the cheeks. In some instances the tongues of several persons have been sewed together.

During all such demonstrations the utmost precaution must be observed. Never under any circumstances mutilate the subject's body by such performances without first obtaining his consent in the presence of a third party before he is placed under the hypnotic influence.

The sewing of tongues together is of too great risk to be performed for mere sensational effect; the least misstep or fall of one of the subjects might cause the most serious consequences under such circumstances.

Before inserting needles or other instruments into hypnotized persons, be sure that such articles are rendered aseptic by first immersing them in some good aseptic fluid.

Seeing is believing in all such cases, and the most skeptical persons readily realize the powers of hypnotism when they personally view the production of anaesthesia in subjects placed under its influence, and anyone who witnesses such exhibitions can the more readily be induced to submit himself to hypnosis when it is necessary for him to be operated upon.

# CHAPTER XVIII.

## HYPNOTISM AND THE INSANE.

Maniacs not easily hypnotized—Melancholia—Weak-minded persons not good subjects—Hypnotism the rational method of curing insanity—Concentration of thought—Insane on the subject of perpetual motion—Case of Mr. Williams—Pacifying a maniac—Insanity from bad habits cured—Religious insanity—Organic diseases must be recognized—Overcoming imaginary notions.

Persons who are violently insane cannot, as a rule, be readily hypnotized, because it is a very difficult matter to force them to concentrate their thoughts upon any one object for any length of time. But those who are suffering from melancholia or other undemonstrative forms of insanity can be much more readily managed.

Many persons have an idea that the weak minded can be easily hynotized, and that good hypnotic subjects have "a screw loose somewhere." This is far from the truth, and the facts in relation to it have been fully given in the chapter on "Qualifications of a Subject."

When it is possible to concentrate the thoughts of an insane person upon some object devised or

selected for the purpose, then hypnosis may be produced and great benefit derived from suggestions.
In fact, hypnotism presents the only rational method
of curing the insane.　Their trains of thought have,
as a rule, traversed one channel in the brain so
intensely that they are beyond ordinary influences
to change them.　Could the mind be rendered passive, then the current of thought could be shifted;
and the frequent repetitions of this would probably result in cure in cases where the structures of
the brain have not been destroyed.

A gentleman of great mechanical ingenuity
became insane upon the subject of perpetual motion.
He had employed all his spare moments for several
years in trying to devise an instrument which his
imagination had conceived, and finally he became
unfit for business and devoted his entire time to his
useless task, at times becoming quite violent at his
inability to accomplish his purpose.　Having no
means, his family soon suffered, and were about
to take steps to confine him in an asylum, when the
author suggested hypnotic influence.

The ordinary methods were evidently useless, and
the following plan was adopted:

He was asked to explain the general principle
of his machine and was given the closest attention.
In every respect he was led to believe that the greatest interest was being manifested in his work, and
various suggestions were made to him from time

to time.  Finally some such remarks as the following were made:

"Mr. Williams, there is only one way in which you can complete your invention, and that is to put yourself in a hypnotic condition and in that way make your mind perfectly passive, so that suggestions will come to you."

He knit his brows a while, evidently in deep thought, and then exclaimed: "All right! I am ready; let us begin at once."

A bright yellow orange was selected as the object upon which he should gaze for the sake of concentration, and it served most effectually.

"Look at this orange," he was told; "it looks like the moon.  It is round and yellow and bright.  If you look at it steadily you will get drowsy and go to sleep.  Look at it, now, and keep on looking at it.  You are drowsy; you are going to sleep; you are asleep—sound, sound asleep."

He was, indeed, sound asleep, and when in the fifth degree of hypnosis (the somnambulistic state), it was suggested to him, most emphatically, that his invention was before him.  He was directed to work at it, and then he was told that one thing was needed: a brass screw half an inch long to connect two wooden bars.  He was made to believe that he supplied and adjusted the screw.  Then he was told that the president was in front of him wishing to see the invention, which he took delight in imagining he was showing.  Then the president told him he must keep the whole thing secret, that he must not work at it any more, and that it would be presented to congress for a suitable reward. After he had agreed to these propositions he was awakened with the precaution: "Don't forget; you will not talk of your invention again."

It seems remarkable, but improvement was noticed at once. He assumed an air of mystery and great secrecy, but did not mention his invention and did not even enter the room he had used for a workshop. He talked rationally, and in few days requested to be hypnotized again. His request was complied with, and it was then suggested that he would not think of his invention until congress sent him the reward. He is probably still waiting for the official notification that shall enrich him. The evidences of insanity have nearly all left him, he never talks of his invention directly, but frequently says: "Some of these days I may be able to count my millions, and I have good reasons for thinking so," or some similar hint of expected riches. He attends to business and is earning a living, although his companions regard him as somewhat highstrung and indisposed to associate with them.

A few years ago an attempt was being made to remove to an ambulance a woman who was violently insane. She resisted every effort and caused quite a struggle. One of the attendants, who was a hypnotist, succeeded in attracting her attention and then commanded her to keep silent and then to go sound asleep. She obeyed, and was placed in the ambulance without further trouble.

The milder cases of insanity, such as are formed by bad habits, are usualy curable by hypnosis and suggestion. They are more fully mentioned in the chapter on "Overcoming Habits by Hypnotism."

Religious insanity, so-called, is often most deplorable, and persons suffering from it are frequently placed in asylums without there being any necessity for doing so. In fact, "religious insanity" is seldom anything more than a concentration of the mind upon one train of thought, and may be completely overcome through hypnotism. It is really not insanity at all, and is often but a symptom of some organic disease, most frequently indicating liver or uterine derangements. Proper treatment of these organs usually suffices to effect a cure, although hypnotic suggestion will more quickly relieve the distressing frame of mind so often mistaken for insanity.

To relieve this trouble, place the subject in the somnambulistic state and impress upon the mind that an angel is present who is making just such statements as the subject should believe. This may be repeated several times and will always have the desired effect. It is a wonderful relief for the family, as well as the patient, to have those fears and notions termed "religious insanity" expelled. As a rule, the patient realizes that they are all imaginary notions, and wishes to overcome them.

# CHAPTER XIX.

## HYPNOTIZING ANIMALS.

Hypnotic power possessed by animals—Hypnotizing animals—Training dogs and horses—Teaching tricks to dogs—Trained elephants—Bringing wild animals under subjection—Man the god of animals—Producing lethargy in frogs—snake charmers—Experiments with rabbits—Hypnotizing roosters and pigeons.

Many animals posses natural hypnotic powers, and exercise them over other animals that are their physical inferiors. Snakes and reptiles usually hypnotize and render motionless their victims before seizing them, and all through the animal kingdom we can realize hypnotic influence being manifested, apparently with studied intent, on the part of the animals exerting the influence.

It is also well known that animals may be easily hypnotized by human beings and made to pass through all the degrees of hypnosis. The training of dogs, horses and other animals is accomplished wholly through hypnotic influence. The animal is usually rendered passive through fear or by riveting its attention upon the eye of the operator, and then emphatic suggestions are made. Take, for instance, the common method of training a dog to sit upright and "beg," which may be accomplished by even a small boy. He places the dog in the required position and points his finger at it and compels it to look steadily. The dog's eyes become fixed on the finger, and as long as they remain so he will obey when commanded to "Sit still, now; steady, steady," etc. In a short time the mere pointing of the finger or the command to "Beg, sir," will insure prompt obedience.

Some of the most marvelous actions are performed by trained animals. Dogs climb ladders and leap through the air, ride horseback, walk on their fore feet with the back feet in the air, and do things that are at entire variance with a dog's natural abilities.

Expert animal trainers have accomplished wonders in this line of work, and the results of their labors are often astounding. Probably the most wonderful performing animals ever exhibited are those trained by the renowned horse trainer, Prof. John O'Brien. Thoroughbred horses of high spirit and great beauty in large numbers go through evolutions of the most difficult character, wholly incongruous with their nature, and do so with an exactness that rivals and supersedes the best trained human actors. Clumsy elephants stand upon their heads, climb ladders, sit upon stools, play the parts of policemen and robbers, perform upon musical instruments, and do innumerable other tricks without the least hesitation, at the mere suggestions of their trainers, who control them with an ease that is marvelous.

The readiness with which fierce animals can be brought to subjection is probably due to the fact that they all naturally stand in awe of human beings, whom they apparently regard as savages do their gods. In some there is a desperate resistance to what they seem to realize must eventually conquer them.

It is not intended here to describe the art of training animals, but a few words regarding the production of the deeper stages of hypnosis will be appropriate.

Frogs may be rendered lethargic by gently rubbing the back, from the head downward. While the frog is being firmly, yet gently, held by one hand, the tips of the fingers of the other hand should rub the back. During an exhibition it will afford great amusement and establish the confidence of the audience to have a box of large frogs on hand, and then, one by one, put them in the lethargic stage and place them in a row upon a table. It is an ocular demonstration that hypnotism is a reality, when even frogs can be influenced.

Snake charmers, by constant and gentle strokes, keep the most venomous reptile in a semi-stupor and render them harmless.

Take upon the stage half-a-dozen rabbits. Draw a chalk-line upon the floor, and, one by one, stroke the rabbits upon the back and lay them along the line, taking care to press each one firmly upon the floor while holding his head in such a position that its eyes will be fascinated by the white line. This experiment will be greatly appreciated, especially if the rabbits are placed in a straight line and are alternately white and black. Roosters and pigeons may be similarly treated.

# CHAPTER XX.

## HYPNOTISM IN BUSINESS AND SOCIETY.

The successful business man—Driving a bargain—Executive ability—Controlling employes—Soliciting insurance—Canvassing—Auctioneering—The air of prosperity—Diplomacy—Social popularity—Entertainers—A brilliant hostess—Aristocracy—Influence of money and titles—Assuming wealth—Consciousness of incapacity—Mental superiority—Compelling recognition—Losing his grip—In the swim.

The successful business man gains his success by his powers to influence others, and he is recognized as an "influential" citizen by all who know him. After he has proven himself to be successful, he exerts a still greater influence upon others, and in that manner he exemplifies the old saying that "nothing succeeds like success."

If we should analyze the characteristics of men who have accumulated wealth, we would realize that they are such characteristics as are enumerated as the qualifications of a hypnotist, namely: Self-confidence, determination to succeed, exercise of will power, fearlessness, concentration of thought, quick perceptive powers, self-possession. Having these powers. the successful business man. whether consciously or unconsciously, exerts hypnotic influence over those with whom he has business dealings.

DRIVING A BARGAIN—It is not everyone who can drive a good bargain, but those who can do so must be able to exercise the power of mentally compelling others to yield to them. A good salesman studies how to influence his customers and to lead their minds to entertain his thoughts and act upon his suggestions. Very frequently we see men of small ability driving shrewd bargains with men of intellect by methods that exert a species of hypnotic influence. They will repeat over and over again, in a loud and tiresome voice, the good qualities of their wares, and by looks and gestures rivet attention upon themselves, and finally succeed in securing a high price for a poor article from a customer who will acknowledge afterward that he was "completely taken in."

EXECUTIVE ABILITY.—Some men find it impossible to control others and make complete failure in any attempt to superintend or oversee subordinates. Other men possess to a remarkable degree the power of controlling employes and are capable of directing great undertakings with simplicity and exactness. Such men are said to possess "executive ability," which is simply another term for a form of hypnotic power.

SOLICITING INSURANCE.—-There is probably no better field in business for the display of hypnotic power than is afforded to the solicitor of insurance.

His subject, when adroitly handled, gives excellent opportunity for guiding the thoughts of his clients and for mentally compelling them to sign applications. The same may be said of canvassing. Let those who are engaged in those occupations study carefully the science of hypnotism, and they will be able to greatly increase their business success.

AUCTIONEERING —Those who are engaged in the business of auctioneering readily comprehend the importance of mental influence. They quickly learn to recognize their ability to guide the thoughts and actions of others. Study the methods of successful auctioneers and you will realize that they are similar to the methods of controlling the actions of others through hypnotism. Even the rapid repetitions in crying out the prices offered are analagous to the monotonous tones of the hypnotist. Attention is first riveted upon the article offered for sale, and, when bidding is once started, the expert auctioneer, by suggestion and mental influence and will power, is enabled to largely control the sale successfully.

THE AIR OF PROSPERITY.—The fact that our mental conditions exert a decided influence upon others is well illustrated in many of the ordinary transactions of life. It is true that the quality of the clothes worn and the words employed in conversation usually have their effect upon others, but a more powreful influence is exerted by mental impulses. A man in shabby clothing may carry about with him an air of prosperity that will secure the confidence of everyone in his ability and financial integrity, while another man, dressed in faultless attire, may display an air of poverty that will inspire only distrust.

Success can never come to the man who continually employs a "hang-dog" manner in all that he says and does. The man who is "dead broke" and broods over the fact will have great difficulty in securing a loan of a dollar from his best friends, while the man who is simply "short on cash" and yet puts on a bold front and carries an air of prosperity or even of self-confidence, usually finds no difficulty in borrowing large sums of money from friends and strangers. But when a man is free from debt and ordinarily prosperous, then is the time to display the air of prosperity that exerts such an influence in financial matters. Learn to control your mental emotions, smother dejecting thoughts, and force yourself to manifest at all times that spirit which is best calculated to win the confidence of others.

DIPLOMACY.—A diplomat is one who can exert a powerful mental influence upon others. In order to succeed in diplomacy, all the qualifications of a hypnotist must be studied and practiced. These are given in Chapter II. Personal magnetism has always been an important factor in private and in state negotiations, and he who can exert the greatest hypnotic influence over the others interested in a transaction is likely to prove the most successful.

SOCIAL POPULARITY—In society personal magnetism always brings popularity. Some persons possess a peculiar mental influence that demands homage from all. In college some one student will be picked out from the rest by his classmates and given a sort of hero worship. As a rule, he is no better student than the rest, and if his character and deeds should be analyzed, nothing remarkable would be found to call for any special recognition, yet he is "the most popular man in college." He possesses that indescribable personal magnetism that is so essential to social success. The student of hypnotism, if he should desire to do so, can cultivate those characteristics and manners that are indispensable to popularity.

ENTERTAINERS —The secret of entertaining lies in the ability to concentrate the thoughts of others upon the conversation or objects presented for entertainment. A lecturer must "have his audience with him" if he desires attention and appreciation. Follow the principles of hypnotism during your endeavors to entertain others, and success will follow. First be full of the subject you desire to present; be oblivious to all surroundings and be possessed with the one idea of presenting your thoughts forcibly and that you have the will power to hold your audience in close attention. Forget self and focus your mind upon your hearers. A good hypnotist will have no difficulty in entertaining others when he desires to do so.

A BRILLIANT HOSTESS —Social functions are rendered most enjoyable when the hostess is an adept in the art of entertaining. She can become such only as she studies the various methods of mentally influencing her guests. A brilliant hostess once remarked: "I owe my success to a determination to make all my guests enjoy themselves. I make them understand that they come to my house for pleasure, and then I strive my best to exercise hypnotic control over them and make enjoyment contagious, and it always works successfully."

ARISTOCRACY —There are certain classes of persons who have a realizing sense of superiority, and deport themselves accordingly. Wealth, ancestral pre-eminence and titles usually beget this feeling of superiority, and although contrary to democratic ideas, it exerts its influence upon the great mass of people in America, as well as in foreign lands. A true aristocrat, with refinement of feelings and capabilities of intellect, is recognized everywhere by unmistakable evidences of mental character which display themselves even in spite of poverty and shabby clothes. Upon the other hand, persons of coarse nature, with suddenly acquired riches, may vainly endeavor, by gaudy display and self-emulation, to impress their superiority upon others. Their shallowness betrays itself because they are unable to mentally experience the feeling of superiority they endeavor to manifest.

ASSUMING WEALTH —In the chapter on

"Self-Hypnotism" instances are given where the constant dwelling upon certain imaginations renders them apparently real. This is often true in regard to wealth. Persons of no means may so continually picture themselves as possessing riches that eventually they will settle down to the belief that they are actually wealthy, and only awaiting the settlement of certain estates until they can assert themselves. We frequently see this in persons who are descendants of the original "beneficiaries" of the "French claims" or of estates in litigation a hundred or more years ago. This delusion of wealth is a species of self-hypnotism that engenders idleness, detraction from useful thoughts and a general false idea of life.

Many worthless and poverty-stricken foreigners, indolent and immoral in habits, are actual or imaginary heirs to titles and estates, and attempt to live accordingly. These vagabonds, who upon their own personal merits and habits would be debarred from associating with decent persons, are freqnently lionized by society and received with open arms into many of the most select family circles. They first hypnotize themselves until their imaginary superiority becomes a living reality, and then they hypnotize others into the same frame of mind. The glamor of empty titles has a mental influence such as is exercised by the various objects hypnotists use in bringing their subjects under hypnotic control.

CONSCIOUSNESS OF INCAPACITY—One

of the greatest drawbacks to business success is the consciousness of incapacity. Circumstances beyond individual control often prevent men from securing more than a limited education or from learning the details of business. They are therefore placed under a disadvantage, and should study every method that offers an opportunity for self-advancement. To realize incapacity and to betray that incapacity is fatal to success. By individual effort deficiencies must be kept in the background. Every man may become proficient in some one direction, and that proficiency must be impressed upon others.

In many instances mental superiority fails to be recognized simply because its possessor is extremely modest and retiring. As a rule, however, superior mental capacity compels recognition. There is an indescribable air of ability that immediately distinguishes a person who possesses mental power and erudition. This cannot long be falsely assumed, neither can it be long concealed; but when actual mental superiority exists it can be used to great personal and general advantage through the medium of hypnotic influence.

Losing His Grip.—We frequently hear the expression, "That man has lost his grip." It implies business failure and mental inability to overcome discouragements. A man who "loses his grip" carries about with him that air of dejection that only increases his failure. It is of the utmost importance that the mind should be trained to withstand discouragements and reverses, for the man who looks upon the dark side of life will be unable to exert any favorable influence over others; in fact, his acknowledgment of defeat and his lack of self-confidence is certain to mentally influence others to refuse him help or to repose confidence in him.

How different is it with the man who is "in the swim." Everything seems to favor him, and what is termed "good luck" apparently follows him everywhere. His mind is in that condition of self-confidence and self-satisfaction that exerts an influence of a similar character over others.

These various phases of mental condition are enumerated for the purpose of illustrating the unconscious influence we can exert. Knowing these statements to be true, we can readily realize the great advantages to be gained by training the mind as we would preparatory to becoming proficient in the art of hynotism.

# CHAPTER XXI.

## HYPNOTISM IN THE PROFESSIONS.

Professional success impossible without hypnotic powers—Personal magnetism—Popularity and success—Hypnotism and the law—Pleading before judge and jury—Criminal lawyers —Following hypnotic methods—Hypnotism an acknowledged aid in curing disease—Securing patients a necessity —Hypnotic power and medical ability—Securing the confidence of patients—Using every means to aid nature—Mental influence—Faith curists—Christian scientists—An ideal practice of medicine—The physician's presence an inspiration—Medical and financial success—Hypnotism and the ministry—How to compel acceptance of church doctrines— Schools of oratory and elocution—Successful preaching.

When we remember that hypnotism is the science and art of mentally controlling thoughts and actions of others, we can realize the great value it possesses to those who employ it in the practice of the various professions. In fact, there can be no great professional success without the practical use of this marvelous power.

When we use the term "personal magnetism," everyone realizes its value as an aid to success and is ready to concede that those who possess it are certain to succeed in the professions. Personal magnetism is simply one form of hypnotism, for it is

the mental power by which others are influenced.
Some men possess it naturally, and their careers
are marked by popularity and success. Some men
acquire it by force of circumstances or deliberate
practice.

In the law hypnotic power is invaluable, and every
lawyer should exercise it whenever opportunity presents itself. Successful lawyers do this, whether
knowingly or not. Notice the method of an attorney
pleading for his client before judge and jury. First
he rivets their attention, usually by a naturally dra-
matic posture, or perhaps by some personal physical characteristics. Next he casts a searching glance
at all and conveys the impression by that glance
that he is deeply in earnest. Then, after securing
the concentration of the judge's and jurymen's
thoughts upon himself, he commences his plea, not
in a suppliant manner, as though the jurymen were
his superiors, from whom he was begging mercy,
but as though he himself were master of the situation. He forces his earnest convictions upon them,
and by emphatic suggestions he influences their
minds not infrequently to bring in a verdict at complete variance with the facts set forth by the testi-
mony.

All noted criminal lawyers are men of great hypnotic power, and they gain their reputations by their
constant use of this power. It is needless to hope
for success in the law without the ability of mentally influencing the thoughts of others, and to do

this most effectively the philosophy of hypnotism must be studied and its methods constantly practiced.

In medicine hypnotism has a wonderful field of usefulness. Its value in treating disease, after patients have been placed under its profound influence, has been mentioned elsewhere. But while the cure of disease is the paramount object of every true physician, the business success of his calling is nevertheless a necessity, and he must secure patients upon whom to practice his skill. Many physicians of undoubted ability can scarcely keep their souls and bodies together on account of their lack of patients upon whom they can demonstrate their ability. Other physicians of little skill and limited knowledge are often seen accumulating wealth in spite of their poor medical success.

It is readily admitted that personal magnetism, or hypnotic power, plays an important part in a physician's career, and when he possesses this, along with medical knowledge and ability, it is possible for him to do great good in the world, and at the same time enjoy a comfortable income.

It is imperative that the physician should secure the confidence of his patients. Let him study their individual characteristics and become such an expert in reading the peculiarities of others that he can at once realize the best method of winning their confidence. If he cannot do this, he might as well abandon the practice of medicine and accept inevitable defeat while it is yet time to make a living in some other calling. The practice of medicine becomes a delight to the physician who realizes his own power to diagnose disease and who has studi‐ously acquired medical knowledge and who has the faculty of securing the implicit confidence of his patients in his ability.

In the cure of disease everything and anything must be employed that will aid the natural efforts being made toward the restoration of health. Among the means of cure, mental influence, or hypnotic power, is or great importance. In many diseases of a nervous character it is all-sufficient, and by its use the Faith Curists, Christian Scientists and others are often enabled to restore health after the most approved use of "powerful drugs" has failed. It is evident that when this mental influence can be called in to aid the actions produced by truly sanative reme‐dies, we have the ideal practice of medicine.

The physician's presence in the sick room should be an inspiration to the patient. In his office his word should be regarded as final and his advice accepted as invariably right. If he actually possesses medical knowledge, he can, by acquiring a knowl‐edge of hypnotism, insure for himself mediical and financial success.

### IN THE MINISTRY.

Why is it that one man preaches to a large and enthusiastic congregation, while another man, per‐haps more profoundly educated and more sincerely devout, cannot bring together a sufficient audience to overcome the emptiness of the chapel? It is because the one possesses personal magnetism, or hypnotic power, and the other does not. One knows how to concentrate the thoughts of his hearers and to lead them along by his suggestions and declarations; the other fails to grasp this important accomplishment.

If it is for the welfare of the human race that the doctrines of churches should be accepted by mankind; then it becomes the duty of every minister and priest to solve the secret of how to mentally compel the acceptance of the doctrines he preaches.

In schools of oratory and of elocution it is the sole purpose to teach how to impress those whom we address, how to attract their attention and how to cause them to become our enthusiastic and appreciative listeners and how to convince them by our words and arguments. In fact, successful preaching and successful oratory, of whatever nature, depend upon hypnotic power, and members of the legal, theological and other professions, whose success depends largely upon oratorical power, should become earnest students of hypnotism.

# CHAPTER XXII.

## GENERAL HYPNOTIC INFLUENCE.

Lasting impressions made upon passive minds—Learning to spell—Expectancy a hypnotic influence—Seeking pleasure —Determined to be gloomy—"Sunset Cox" and his postponed lecture—Public gatherings—Spirit of the meeting—Magnetic speakers—Hypnotic power necessary to successful public speaking—Powerful preachers—All more or less obedient—Sleight of hand exhibitions—Oriental magicians —An East India exhibition—Hypnotized through objects.

All persons are more or less influenced by others, whether consciously or unconsciously. When the mind is comparatively passive, then it receives impressions more readily, and those impressions are usually very lasting. A child can learn to spell correctly because of this fact, and he will remain a correct speller. But an adult who is a poor speller will have great difficulty in acquiring correctness. For the same reason, all through life, even to old age, a person may vividly remember trifling occurrences that made a vivid impression upon his mind during childhood.

Expectancy likewise exerts an emphatic hypnotic influence upon the mind. "Those see best who desire to see" is an old saying. Travelers often go into raptures while looking upon the scenery of the mountains or valleys of which they have read descriptions, while equally beautiful scenery at home does not even attract their attention. It is anticipation that renders the actual realization most enjoyable.

Pleasure parties setting out with the determination to enjoy themselves will be able to take delight in the most commonplace occurrences, and on the other hand a person determined to see nothing of interest anywhere will find himself gloomy and morose even in the midst of pleasures.

An incident well illustrating the influence of expectancy is related of the late Hon. S. S. Cox, well known as "Sunset Cox," the congressman and humorist. At one time he was announced to deliver a comic lecture in a Pennsylvania city, and before the hour arrived the hall was crowded to overflowing with persons who had come anticipating a feast of laughter.

Just before the curtain should arise Mr. Cox was given a telegram announcing the sudden death of his wife's mother at his home in New York City. He was greatly shocked by the news and told the manager it would be impossible for him to deliver his lecture under the circumstances. After a brief conference it was decided that Mr. Cox should step in front of the curtain and state the facts to the audience and announce that the lecture would be postponed for one week. He accordingly proceeded to the front of the stage and was received with vociferous applause. After this had subsided he said:

"Ladies and Gentlemen: I hold in my hand a telegram, just received, announcing the death of my mother-in-law"——

His voice was then drowned by uproarious laughter. It was the period when "the mother-in-law joke" was going the rounds, and the audience took it for granted that Mr. Cox was introducing his lecture in the most comical manner, and his apparent solemnity seemed to be so well feigned that it added to their appreciation. He stood for some moments, dazed by the unexpected reception of his words, until it dawned upon him that they had mistaken his announcement for a joke. When quiet was restored he proceeded:

"Friends, my statement is a solemn fact. The telegram is from my home in New York City. My mother-in-law made her home with me, and I dearly loved her. It is with feelings of great grief that I learn of her death. Under the circumstances I cannot proceed with my lecture, and it will be postponed until one week from to-night. The audience is now dismissed, and you will receive your tickets upon leaving the hall."

It was amidst laughter and shouts that he managed to say what he did, and when he retired from the stage the applause was deafening. Surely for a humorous lecture there couldn't be a better introduction, and his imitative powers seemed perfect. The audience had come to hear fun and jokes, and Mr. Cox evidently was not going to be a disappointment. Before quiet could be restored the manager was compelled to step forth and emphatically corroborate Mr. Cox's statements.

In public gatherings we are often more influenced by the "spirit of the meeting" than by what has been actually said or done. If we should put into plain English the few words uttered at revival meetings, they might seem commonplace, but in the meeting they "burn with fire" when spoken in the midst of excitement and to receptive minds. A magnetic political speaker can sway his audience by a few threadbare assertions spoken in a convincing manner. By his voice and demeanor he suggests the character of the reception he desires his words to receive.

Speakers and orators would do will to study thoroughly this phase of hypnotic power. It is a valuable acquisition to knowledge and must be possessed in order to make a success of public speaking. Old-time ministers used to sing-song their sermons at the start, and then slowly get warmed up and "cap the climax" by loud and rapid talk and wild gestures. Whoever could do this was accounted "a powerful preacher." It was simply a method of hypnotizing his listeners. He did not call it hypnotism, and perhaps gave little thought to how he managed to work up enthusiasm; but, regarded in the light of hypnotic science, it was identical with modern methods of mentally controlling others. First, the mind anticipates being influenced; second, the quietude of the surroundings, with concentration of thought upon what is about to be said; third, the monotonous sound of the "sing-song" voice; fourth, the emphatic suggestion.

We are all more or less obedient to others, and under certain circumstances we implicitly obey without question. This fact is well illustrated by our behavior in public. For instance, at a "sleight-of-hand" exhibition, the performer depends largely upon the obedience of the audience for his success. The spectators follow his suggestions with unanimity as soon as they are uttered. He says, "Look at the ceiling," and instantly all eyes are turned upward. He commands absolute silence for a moment, and it is promptly secured. In fact, he has announced his intention of doing mysterious things, and everyone present spontaneously aids him in his work. It is this exercise of hypnotic influence that aids the Oriental magician in his performances that sometimes seem to be almost beyond belief, but which his spectators declare they saw with their "very eyes."

The following incident, related by a traveler in Eastern India, is an interesting example of hypnotic influence:

"We had scarcely become comfortable, or, rather, settled, in our apartments in the inn, when a servant announced that a band of magicians were about to give a performance in the courtyard. I had always desired to see such a performance by natives in their own country, and hastened below. Seated on the ground was a man of dark complexion, with a turban about his head and wearing the regulation costume. About him were several other natives, evidently his assistants, one of whom spoke English and acted as interpreter. In front of the magician were several small jars and boxes and other implements pertaining to his calling. It is needless to go into detail as to what was said and done. The performance started with an exhibition of several small snakes taken from one of the boxes. The snakes were undoubtedly real, and as the magician sang a monotonous song and occasionally touched the snakes with a peculiar wand, they became gradually larger and larger, until they assumed the proportions of large boa constrictors and caused consternation among us; then, at a command, they grew smaller, and entered the box from which they had been taken—a box scarcely large enough to hold a pound of tea.

"One of the assistants drew a circle in the sand and stood in the center of it, seeming to take great pains to ascertain just where the exact center was. The magician then touched him and he spun around like a top, and with a shout ascended high into the air and vanished amid the clouds. In a short time he reappeared and fell down upon the spot from whence he started.

"Several other equally remarkable feats were performed, to the details of which being actual occurrences we would have testified. But several of the ladies of our company, who viewed the scene from a concealed balcony, declared that they saw nothing more than ordinary-sized snakes, a man spinning around on one spot, and other simple manifestations. They had been without the sphere of influence, and the rest of us, in some remarkable manner, had been hypnotized and our senses rendered susceptible to spoken and acted suggestions. We saw what did not take place, but that which the operator had willed us to see, and had it not been for the ladies on the balcony we would never have realized that we had been controlled by fascination."

We do not always like to acknowledge hypnotic control; but a few instances will serve to demonstrate that we are all more or less influenced by a peculiar fascination exercised over us by the sight of unusual or suggestive objects.

We cannot watch a tight-rope walker in midair without becoming dizzy or experiencing the sensation of falling.

When standing upon the top of a very high building, the suggestion of jumping off comes to us at once, and many have given way to their impulse and committed suicide who had no intention of doing so. The sight of a very high bridge not infrequently fascinates persons to such an extent that they have been impelled to walk upon it and then jump from it into the river.

Some persons upon a railroad platform have difficulty in keeping themselves from jumping in front of a fast-approaching train. Others cannot handle a revolver without a suggestion coming to them of what destruction it might perform, and without any premeditation and almost involuntarily they are pointing it at themselves or others, and possibly pulling the trigger.

These performances are due to a species of hypnotic influence. The object fascinates and concentrates the thought, which immediately forms the idea and is very frequently instantly transferred to the seat of physical action, with most disastrous although unpremeditated results.

# CHAPTER XXIII.

## POST-HYPNOTISM.

Suggestions carried out after awakening—Somnambulistic state—Practical illustration—Awake at four o'clock in the morning—Post-hypnotic suggestions always obeyed—Honorable persons will not commit crime by post-hypnotic suggestion—Keeping an appointment—Unable to eat his Sunday dinner—Cannot drink tea or coffee—Overcoming the liquor habit—Post-hypnotic suggestion a great power for good or evil—Valuable in treating nervous conditions—Changing personal likes and dislikes—As an aid for self-control—Avoiding evil companions—Hypnotism cannot change a person's moral nature—Affairs of the heart —Had her sweetheart hypnotized—A parent's use of hypnotism.

One of the most interesting and valuable of all hypnotic phenomena is that of post-hypnotic suggestion. This is the suggestion made to the hypnotized subject which he carries out at some future time designated by the operator when the suggestion is made. The time designated may be hours, days or months after the subject has been awakened, and yet the act will be performed as suggested when the time arrives.

In order to be successful in making post-hypnotic suggestions, the operator must first place the sub-

ject in profound hypnosis—the condition of somnambulism being best.  When this state has been
reached, passess must be made over the body and
suggestion uttered in a most emphatic manner.  By
way of example, the following illustration will
prove interesting:

A young man who had allowed himself to be
hypnotized for amusement was brought into the
somnambulistic state.  After several ordinary experiments had been conducted, it was decided to make
a post-hypnotic suggestion.  Accordingly he was
"mesmerized" by passes from the head to the feet
and rendered profoundly hypnotized.  Standing
beside him, the operator said:

"Harry, to-morrow morning you will wake up
at four o'clock, and you will not be able to sleep
after that time, and every morning for a week you
will wake up at the same time and dress yourself
and stay awake till evening.  Now, you will not
remember that I told you this, but you will do it,
without fail, for you simply can't help yourself."

Such words were repeated emphatically to him several times, and then he was awakened.  The next
day he surprised himself and others by awakening
just as the hands of the clock indicated the hour of
four, and each morning for a week he did the same
thing.  The eighth morning he slept soundly until
a late hour.

It makes no difference what post-hypnotic suggestion is made to the subject while in the som-

nambulistic state, if properly made he will obey it strictly, provided it does not call for the performance of an act repulsive to his nature. Honorable men cannot be made to commit crime by post-hypnotic suggestion, much as criminals would like to declare otherwise. Nevertheless, a man willing to do a criminal act may have the act suggested to him by post-hypnotic suggestion, and he will perform it at the time designated. It is possible that the actual perpetrator of the deed would not be responsible under such circumstances, but until the phenomena of hypnotism are more generally understood, it will be difficult to settle the legal aspects of such cases satisfactorily.

Make the post-hypnotic suggestion to a subject that one month from date he will call at your office bareheaded, and he will certainly do it at that time, although he will be at a loss to explain his action.

Suggest that a subject will be unable to eat his dinner on the following Sunday, and he will have no appetite at that time; or, suggest that he will find himself unable to enjoy tea or coffee or alcoholic liquors of any kind, and the dislike for them will follow. Of course, it will require oft-repeated post-hypnotic suggestions to accomplish the permanent dislike for liquors; but it can be done, and all bad habits can be overcome in this manner, provided the mind is not destroyed by long indulgence. More upon this subject will be found in the chapter on "Overcoming Habits by Hypnotism."

A great power for good or evil lies in post-hypnotic suggestion. It is the key to curing many diseases and correcting mental peculiarities. It is an invaluable aid, especially in nervous conditions, and many cases of hysteria have been permanently cured by warding off periodical attacks through post-hypnotism.

There is another phase of post-hypnotic suggestion that should be recognized, and that is its power to affect the life of individuals. Persons may be made to completely change their personal likes and dislikes of others. In some instances this is desirable, but it is not always right. A few authentic cases will illustrate the practical uses of this peculiar exercise of hypnotic influence.

A father brought his son to the office for treatment to overcome a lack of self-control. He was a young man of good education and always enjoyed every advantage of life. His family were refined and wealthy, and not only highly respectable, but sincerely religious. He himself was inclined to live a moral life, but could not withstand the temptations presented to him by his companions. These companions had been his playmates in childhood, and it was difficult, and, in fact, impossible, for him to refuse to associate with them, although they were continually leading him into trouble, or, at least, into performing acts that were at variance with his sense of proper living, and which occasioned his parents much anxiety.

He was willing and anxious to test the power of hypnotism as an aid for giving him what he termed "strength of character." Accordingly, he was hypnotized by the usual method and placed in the somnambulistic state. He was then told that it would be impossible for him to be induced to accompany his friends to any questionable places, and that whenever they met him he would treat them civilly, but would no longer make companions of them. Over and over again these suggestions were emphatically repeated to him before he was awakened, and this was repeated daily for twelve days, during which time he had no communication with any of his companions, as his father had brought him quite a distance to secure the benefits of this hypnotic treatment.

Upon his return home the post-hypnotic suggestions were strictly carried out. He met his former companions and treated them with civility, but he absolutely refused to enter into any of their plans for having a "good time." They soon took offense at his coolness toward them, and ceased to associate with him. He considered the hypnotic treatment had given him strength of character, for he had no recollection of the post-hypnotic suggestions. But hypnotic treatment did not give him strength of character. It cannot change a person's nature. The post-hypnotic suggestions were carried out because they were not at variance with his sense of right and wrong. In fact, they were more easily carried out because they were what he most desired to do.

A couple of cases of "affairs of the heart," which read almost like fairy stories, with a wizard to "throw a spell" over the lovers, are here given as actual occurrences, which may be repeated whenever necessity dictates:

It is said that the course of true love never does run smooth, and this was the case with Miss Edith. She was engaged to marry a young man who had succeeded in securing her utmost devotion. Being of a decidedly jealous nature, she became miserable in mind when she realized that he was on many occasions very attentive to her own cousin. It seemed to her that the cousin would surely win him from her, and she devised all manner of means to keep her cousin out of his thoughts, but without avail. Finally, after witnessing, with her lover, an exhibition of hypnotism, she privately called on the hypnotist and consulted him in regard to the matter, and was encouraged to challenge her lover to be hypnotized. He accepted the challenge and was completely hypnotized, and while under the influence the suggestion was made to him that he would at a certain time call upon the young lady rival and upbraid her for some oversight in a manner that would give offense. The post-hypnotic suggestion acted like a charm, and there was no longer any cause for jealousy.

An incident is related where a father was very

much worried about his daughter's evident love for a worthless suitor. Being a young and romantic girl, and a great reader of novels, the father could not believe the love to be more than of a sentimental nature. Persuasion and commands being of no avail, he consulted an expert hypnotist and arranged for a private exhibition in his own home. He persuaded the daughter to be hypnotized, and while in the somnambulistic state post-suggestions were made to her calculated to disrupt the affectionate relationship distasteful to her parents. The plan worked well. The girl became interested in hypnotism and frequently subjected herself to its influence, and each time she was hypnotized posthypnotic suggestions were made to her, which led to abhorrence of the worthless suitor.

The above case probably would not have been so successful from the parents' standpoint, if, instead of sentimentalism, earnest and steadfast love had existed; for it is almost impossible to uproot deep affection through hypnotic influence.

# CHAPTER XXIV.

## AWAKENING A SUBJECT.

Mistaken belief—Subject can always be awakened—Accidental
injury or death of the operator—Extreme lethargic condition—Common method of awakening—Display of alarm—
No harm from delayed awakening—Lethargic subjects
awaken slowly—Blowing upon the neck—Sleeping all day
—Suggestions of the operator—Not awakened suddenly
from somnambulism—Pleasant suggestions before awakening.

A great many persons entertain the idea that a
hypnotized subject might possibly fail to awaken
under the commands of the operator, and that serious consequences would then follow. This thought
is often uppermost in the minds of those who desire
to be hypnotized and yet hesitate, and it is also
entertained by many who are entering upon the
study of hynotism with the desire of becoming
operators.

There is nothing whatever to fear in connection
with awakening from hypnosis. A subject who
has been placed in the hypnotic condition can always
be awakened by the operator who hypnotized him,
and the operator will always be able to awaken him,
unless, of course, he should himself be overcome
by a stroke of paralysis or other accident, when

the subject would, even then, awaken of his own accord, the time of awakening being in accordance with the degree of hynosis. There is one remote exception to this rule. It is possible for a subject to be put in the extreme lethargic condition, or a state of death-like trance, and to be told by the operator, "You cannot possibly awaken without my awakening you." Then, indeed, we might fear evil consequences might follow if the operator should die or become paralyzed before awakening his subject.

The most common method of releasing a subject from hypnosis is for the operator to snap the fingers close to the subject's ears and sharply command him to "Wake up! wake up! Now you are awake! You're all right!" In nearly every case this will suffice to make the subject give a start and look about him in a confused manner for a moment or so, and then smile and probably make some such remark as "Yes, I am awake."

If from any reason the subject does not awaken at once by such an action, then it should be repeated a little more sharply. But never under any circumstances should the operator manifest the least alarm or discomfiture if there should be delay. No possible harm is going to happen, and the awakening will soon be complete. Occasionally the awakening from the cataleptic, somnambulistic or lethargic stages may be rather slow. To hasten it, blow a quick, short breath through the puckered mouth upon the neck of the subject. This will have the desired effect.

It may happen that the operator has told the somnambulist that "You will sleep all day," and then he might experience difficulty in awakening him before evening. It is, therefore, important that the operator should exercise reasonable judgment in his remarks and commands. He should remember what he has said, and if at variance with quick awakening, he should contradict it by other remarks, such as "You needn't sleep all day; you will wake up whenever I tell you to do so."

Some operators make it a rule to state to their subjects before awakening them, "Now, I am going to count three, and when I say three you will wake up." This is usually sufficient.

It is always a good plan to have a subject in a light degree of hypnosis before awakening him. For instance, he should not be suddenly awakened from somnambulism, or if the cataleptic stage has been induced, he should be told, "Now you can move your arms freely, and now you are not as sound asleep as you were; you are going to wake up soon." When he is apparently in the early stages of hypnosis again, then tell him, "All right! Wake up!"

To make the subject's experience with hypnotism as pleasant as possible and render him anxious to repeat the experiments, tell him, before awakening him, "You are feeling splendid—Oh! so comfort-

able and happy," and make other similar suggestions. He will usually say, "Yes, I feel very good,
and I am very happy. I wish I could always feel
so good." Then tell him, "Well, while you are
feeling so good I am going to wake you up. All
right! Wake up! wake up!"

# CHAPTER XXV.

## MIND READING—TELEPATHY.

Communication of thought—Natural power—Birds and animals—Thoughts of children—Betraying the emotions—Guilty conscience—Detection of crime—Criminal demeanor—Attracting attention—School recitations—Love and anger—Impressions during sleep—Premonitions—Distance no barrier—Tests—Transmitting thoughts—Phenomenon of clairaudience—How to transmit thoughts.

It is possible to communicate our thoughts to others without words or gestures or physical means of any kind. We can, through the exercise of will power, reveal to others the thoughts we entertain, and we can, through the same power, have revealed to us the thoughts of others, even without their being conscious of the fact.

There is nothing remarkable in the above statement; in fact, this communication of thought without the aid of physical agencies is a natural power, and it is altogether probable that in the earlier stages of existence mankind employed but few sounds to convey his ideas and emotions. The more primitive the race, the smaller is the vocabulary. This is a rule well known by scientists. The savages communicate with one another with very few words, yet they make their wants and emotions known and realize one another's feelings as readily as the most highly educated scholars comprehend the hidden meanings conveyed by a select and large vocabulary.

Savages are not only able to communicate thoughts with very few words, but they are able to comprehend, without any words, the emotions entertained by others. This is true of birds and animals and infants who cannot speak as we do. By some natural power they realize the anger or fear or kindliness we experience toward them whenever we come into their presence.

It is altogether probable that the future will establish a means of communicating thoughts, which will enable experts to largely abolish the use of words. Many persons are unable to prevent the betrayal of their feelings and reveal their inmost emotions as perfectly without words as with them.

A guilty conscience usually betrays itself, and the cause of this well illustrates the method of thought transference. Suppose a criminal has committed a criminal act, and fears detection. His mind constantly dwells upon the possibility of detection, and whenever he comes in contact with others his whole soul is engaged in the thought, "Do they realize what I have done?" Such a thought engaging the mind is quickly transferred to others. It simply cannot be retained. We may call it the escape of concentrated nerve force, or give it any explanation we please, the fact remains the same, and is recognized by all. Criminals are very frequently detected more by their criminal demeanor and their inability to control their mental influence, than by the means of clues and informants.

It is a well-known fact that almost anyone can attract attention by will power. For instance, if in a public gathering you should recognize the presence of a friend in the opposite part of the hall, concentrate your whole mind upon the desire to have him see you; earnestly will that he shall turn about and recognize you. If you are intense in your desire and your exercise of will power, you will have the satisfaction of realizing that your effort is successful.

School children are very often adepts at thought communication. If they have prepared especially well their lessons for the day, they learn to "make the teacher call upon them to recite," and are usually successful. But such children often experience the chagrin of disappointment when not prepared. In such instances their minds are so absorbed in fear lest the teacher should call upon them that they exert a mental influence and involuntarily transfer their thoughts, which results in their often being asked "the very question they were not able to answer."

It needs no philosophy to explain the fact that lovers can sit by the hour in each other's presence and scarcely speak a dozen words, yet be in an

ecstacy of delight, and each realize that the other
is experiencing emotions of profoundest love. These
are the most common and most pleasant instances
of soul transference of thought, and have been
experienced ever since man and woman learned the
first lessons of love.

All the emotions may be similarly made manifest
by thought transference on account of their intensity. Fear, anger, sympathy, passion, indignation,
pity, abhorrence and delight, when intensely experienced, need no words to convey their meaning to
others.

### IMPRESSIONS DURING SLEEP.

During profound sleep, which is natural hypnosis,
the mind may become passive and subject to vivid
impressions, the source of which may be at a great
distance. How frequently do we hear from truth-
ful persons that they were warned in a dream of the
death of a friend or relative, and afterward found
that the death was an actual occurrence. During
the seige of Pekin, a mother whose daughter was
in the beseiged city declared that her daughter
appeared to her in a vision and announced that she
was safe from harm. The vision was so real that
she fully believed in its reality and secured great
comfort.

Premonitions of danger experienced during sleep
are exceedingly frequent, and have been common
to mankind since the earliest times. Who cannot
recall an individual instance where the coming of

a friend or enemy was felt a short time before meeting him? Such an instance demonstrates that the mind knows no barrier of distance. Space is annihilated when the power to transfer thought has been developed. The premonition of coming friends or letters, or the seeing of objects in visions, is known as clairvoyance.

All hypnotists are not necessarily experts in telepathy. In fact, many persons who possess undoubted hypnotic powers are unable to successfully carry on communication of thoughts with others, while, on the other hand, persons who have never hypnotized others may become experts in telepathy.

### HOW TO TRANSMIT THOUGHT.

To successfully practice telepathy, the operator must possess a sound body and an evenly balanced mind, free from bad habits and at peace with all mankind. There must be no emotions or revengeful feelings to mar the tranquility of mind, and he must possess all the qualifications of a hypnotist described in Chapter II.

Confidence of success is of the first importance, and this must be enhanced by the ability to make the mind passive and to concentrate the thought whenever desired. For experimentation it is always best to practice telepathy with some person who has been previously hypnotized by the operator, or who has given evidence of readily being mentally influenced. Also during the first experiments the subject, or recipient, as he is called in this connection, should not be far distant from the operator, or transmitter.

If you have given the subject sufficient study and reflection to inspire confidence in your ability, secure a proper subject and give him the fullest understanding possible of what you desire to do. Select some one who is interested in the topic of telepathy and who is anxious to experiment.

Have the subject or recipient retire to an adjoining room and instruct him to make his mind perfectly passive; also inform him in a general way what is to be the character of your thoughts. For instance, state, "I am going to think of five geographical names," or, "I am going to think of four persons." After he has retired, concentrate your whole mind upon the names or persons you may select, and then will that the subject shall receive your thoughts. Do not be engrossed in a desire that he shall know what you are thinking about, for that desire implies a doubt, which is fatal, as it creates a new train of thought in your mind. Force upon yourself the felling that you are mentally expelling from your mind the thoughts selected, and that you are driving them into the recipient's mind.

Your success in your first experiment will be demonstrated by the subject informing you of the words or persons selected. He may not be able at first to give you the actual words, but may tell you the substance of the thought. For instance, he may say, "You were thinking of a city in China, a river in Europe, one of the United States, one of the great lakes, and an island in the Pacific Ocean," or he may describe the persons that you selected. This may be due to the thoughts which the names called up to your own mind, for the bare name can scarcely be dwelt upon without qualification, unless it be in the case of figures.

After repeated experiments at close range, long-distance communications may be attempted, and they are just as easily and successfully performed when the thought of distance can be banished from the mind.

The author has performed very many most interesting experiments in telepathy with his friend, Mr. Erasmus Poole, a gentleman of high literary and scientific attainments, who has made the study of occult sciences an absorbing specialty.

Mr. Poole, a few years since, made a business trip to Boston, and it was agreed that an experiment at "double telepathy" should be attempted. In other words, that we should act as transmitter and recipient in turn. We agreed upon a day and hour and minute when we should place ourselves in communication. The author was first to transmit, and after a lapse of half an hour was to render his mind passive and receive. What was received in Boston was to be afterward sent by mail to Chicago, together with a written statement of what was sent, and a corresponding communication was to be mailed from Chicago to Boston. The following is the result:

FIRST MESSAGE.

"Boston, January 18th.—In my sitting to-day with you I received the following impressions, like a telegraphic message: 'Very cold; friend very sick; send black book.'"

The message transmitted by telepathy and afterward mailed to Chicago was: "Thermometer nine degrees below zero. Mr. Boettinger has typhoid fever. Please return the book on 'Psychology' you borrowed."

SECOND MESSAGE.

"Chicago, January 18th.—As agreed upon, I made myself passive, after sending you a message, and I received the following mental impressions: 'Time 4136. Smoke everywhere.'"

The actual message, as Mr. Poole afterward informed me by mail, was: "My watch number is 411366. Fire in my boarding house yesterday. Received a letter from Smith."

It is evident that the success of the experiment was quite satisfactory, and although the exact words were not received as transmitted, the thoughts were. In the first message the words "thermometer nine degrees below zero very naturally created the thought of "very cold." The appearance of the book on psychology created the thought of "black book," and the name and disease were absorbed in the thought of "friend very sick."

In the second message all the figures were received correctly, but the repetition of 1 and 6 were not comprehended. The words, "Fire in our boarding house yesterday" created the idea of smoke in the transmitter's mind, which was the thought received, and probably the smoke had made such an impression that the recollection of it precluded the concentration of thought upon the fact of receiving a letter from Smith, which slightly entertained thought was not received at all.

Enough has been learned and demonstrated in regard to telepathy to make it apparent that future generations may reach such a high degree of experience and knowledge regarding it, that it will be a recognized means of communication, just as wireless telegraphy, incomprehensible to most persons, and until lately regarded as impossible by all, has become practical in the sending of actual messages.

# CHAPTER XXVI.

## HYPNOTIC MISCELLANY.

Signs of hypnosis—Fascination—Catalepsy—Lethargy—Exaltation of the senses—Muscular contortions—Singing and speaking—Speaking in foreign languages—At the prize fight—Hunting and fishing—Laughing and crying—Make me a child again—Aged and infirm—Becoming animals—A trip to heaven—Up in a balloon.

Subjects who are being brought into a condition of hypnosis will usually give physical evidence of their being under control. At first the pupils of the eyes will be noticeably contracted, and as the influence becomes intensified they gradually dilate and become very large, and in the profound stages the eyeballs will roll upward, as may be readily seen by lifting the eyelids. If, when in the somnambulistic state, the subject should be required to open his eyes, the eyeballs will usually assume their natural position.

Most subjects, as they fall into the hypnotic state, will show a peculiar smile about the mouth, which by many is mistaken as an evidence of assumed subjection. When slumber results from suggestion, the eyelids are apt to quiver slightly just as they are closing, and the breathing becomes deeper and regular.

FASCINATION—After the subject has been placed in the somnambulistic state by the ordinary method, mentioned elsewhere, some object, a cane, for instance, may be used to fascinate. Attention is called to it in some such manner os follows:

"Look at the head of this cane; fix your eyes upon it, and keep looking at it. Now your eyes are fastened to it, and you can't stop looking at it until I tell you to do so."

The subject will rivet his eyes upon the head of the cane, and if near enough he will seem to be glued to it, and wherever the cane is moved he will follow. He will run after it, jurp in the air to reach it, lie on the floor to be near it, and keep his eyes upon it regardless of all surroundings and all dangers.

The nose of the subject may be mentally fastened to an object in the same manner. When this experiment is performed it is best not to bring the object too close to the eyes, on account of the possibility of eye strain. Care must also be taken to incur no risks from falls or other injuries, as the fascinated subject is entirely oblivious of everything except the object that fascinates him.

Catalepsy.—A favorite demonstration of profound hypnosis made in public exhibitions is the production of catalepsy. The subject is brought into this condition by the method explained in

Chapter VII, and when the subject is perfectly rigid, his body is lifted and placed in such a position as to cause the head to rest upon one chair, while the feet rest upon another, making of it a sort of human bridge, upon which the operator may place weights, or upon which he may stand. Such an act is positive evidence of hypnosis, for it cannot be performed under natural conditions.

Very frequently we hear of large stones being placed upon the chest of a cataleptic person, and then being broken by a sledge hammer. This can be done, but it must be remembered that hypnosis does not alter the structures of bones and muscles, and serious physical injury might follow such an uncalled-for exhibition.

In this connection it is well to repeat the caution against forcing a subject into a lethargic trance except for purely scientific purposes. Operators have rendered their subjects almost lifeless for days and weeks, and in Oriental countries self-hypnotists have thrown themselves into trances lasting for months.

### PUBLIC EXHIBITIONS.

When giving public exhibitions of hypnotic power, it is well to plan beforehand amusing performances that will be positive proofs of hypnotic influence. First put the subject in the somnambulistic state, as directed in Chapter VII, and then, by positive suggestions, any of the following remarkable exhibitions can be made.

All the senses may be exalted to the highest degree, and the subject will give evidence of this in an unmistakable manner. Drop a pin upon the floor with the remark that you are going to drop a cannon ball, and when the pin falls he will jump and manifest a consciousness of having actually heard the falling of a heavy weight.

Suggest that you are going to explode a dynamite bomb. Hold an egg in the hand and state that it is the bomb. Break the egg, and the subject will clap his hands to his ears and show great distress and fright, such as he would manifest should an actual explosion of dynamite occur.

Give the subject a bottle of cologne and tell him he cannot take it away from his nose; then suggest that it is a bottle of strong ammonia, and he will act accordingly. Or give him a peeled onion and suggest that it is a rose, and he will show great delight in holding it to his nostrils.

Dancing, leaping, jumping, and other displays of muscular agility may be made by suggestion. It is a strange fact that many persons who have never danced can be made to do so in the hypnotic state, and will usually perform very gracefully when there is musical accompaniment. Some hypnotists make their subjects contort their bodies by bending backwards or putting the leg over the head, or doing similar difficult exercises. Such performances are dangerous, unless the subject is an acrobat. There are an abundance of harmless and amusing feats to be performed to demonstrate hypnotism without resorting to those that risk life or limb.

Subjects can be made to sing songs or to deliver orations while in the hypnotic condition. Those who are usually backward in doing these things may be greatly benefited by being hypnotized and forced to do them. Such persons may have post-suggestions made to them advantageously. It is not necessary for the operator to think of the words to be spoken. Let the suggestion be made, and results will follow. For instance, say, "You are William Jennings Bryan, and the crowd of people before you want to have you make them a speech on 'Free Silver, 16 to 1.'" It is often surprising to note the display of oratory that will follow such a suggestion. A new subject cannot be relied upon to speak in this manner for the first time, and in a public exhibition only a well-known, good subject should be used.

Expert hypnotists sometimes demonstrate their power of compelling the subject to speak in a foreign tongue with which he is unfamiliar. This is done by previously hypnotizing the subject and repeating to him several times the words you wish him to commit to memory. He will commit them very readily and repeat them whenever he is again hypnotized and called upon to do so. It is, of course, impossible to give a hypnotized subject the power to freely use a foreign language.

Very amusing exhibitions may be made by suggesting to hypnotized subjects that they are fishing or hunting. Give them brooms or pokers or umbrellas for fishing rods, and they will in imagination cast their lines and upon suggestions draw in huge fishes and go through all the maneuvers of fishermen. Give them any articles for guns and set them rabbit hunting; they will take aim and shoot and pick up their imaginary rabbits and skin them and cook them and devour them with evident relish.

The emotions may be easily excited by hypnotic suggestions. A number of subjects thrown into hearty laughter will render their actions contagious to persons in the audience, who will also become convulsed with laughter. This is a good thing to occasionally do, for it puts the audience into good humor. On the other hand, crying and sobbing may be easily induced; but it must be remembered that sudden changes from joy to grief, or vice versa, must not be permitted. Such sudden changes are liable to produce hysterics in nervous subjects during hypnosis.

Probably one of the most amusing and harmless performances during hypnosis is the suggestions made to various subjects that they have grown old, or that they are babes or children. Full-grown men will act with perfection the part of two-year-olds, and children may be made to assume all the attitudes of the aged and infirm. It is amusing to have upon the platform at one time a group of adults playing childish games, with bibs about their necks, while young persons are sedately posing as aged men or women.

Subjects can be made to believe that chairs or tables or other articles of furniture are various animals. A girl will take a silk hat as a bucket and proceed to milk the table as a cow. A man will jump astride a chair and urge his imaginary horse to full speed. Books become cats or dogs or anything else the operator may desire the subject to believe them to be. Again, the subjects themselves may, upon suggestion, assume the role of various animals.

A beautiful exhibition of supreme happiness follows the suggestion to a group of hypnotized subjects that they have taken a trip to heaven and are enjoying its glories. Such a trip may be commenced by suggesting to the party that they are to travel heavenward in a balloon. The caution they will portray and the emotions they will evince become very realistic.

Many more amusing and entertaining performances will suggest themselves to the operator who is giving a public exhibition. In all such exhibitions let the acts blend pleasantly from one to the other. Sudden changes are trying on the subject and also detract from the harmony of the exhibition.

# CHAPTER XXVII.

## SELF-ANAESTHESIA.

Self-anaesthesia a natural power—Exhibited by animals—
Common examples in human beings—Heroism of children—Daughter of Mr. French—Case of Earnest Gunther—
Remarkable power of Hakim Abdel Sureddin—Clinical
experiments.

The power to render the body or portions of it
insensible to pain is probably possessed by all human
beings, although as yet few have been able to
develop it satisfactorily.  It requires great concentration of thought and self-confidence, together with
patient practice.  In many of the lower animals this
power seems to be exercised with the greatest ease,
although whether it is under their self-control or
simply a result of fright and consequent hypnosis,
has not yet been definitely settled.  Some animals
fall into a stupor as soon as they are captured; for
instance, the opossum will curl up as if in profound sleep or dead, when about to be taken;
lobsters will sever portions of their bodies that have
been caught in traps, and many other manifestations
of a peculiar nature in this connection are familiar
to all.  Some persons even go so far as to assert

that as a rule animals do not suffer much pain when subjected to abuse or apparent tortures.

In human beings the endurance of pain differs greatly, and almost instinctively we realize that it is within our power to modify our sufferings. How often we use the expression, "Grin and bear it," or, "I shut my teeth and bore it like a hero," or "he bravely endured the operation without fliniching." There are various directions given for lessening pain, such as, "Grit your teeth," "Think of something else," "Press your fingers in the ears," etc. All these things simply show that to a certain extent our powers are realized and often feebly taken advantage of when most needed. Surely it should become a matter of great interest to us to seek methods of developing this most beneficent attribute of our natures.

Occasionally we notice children displaying wonderful heroism under trying circumstances and becoming almost stoical during the infliction of punishment. The little seven-year-old daughter of Mr. French, of Pendleton, Indiana, was able to control herself in a remarkable manner. When punished or even rebuked for misdemeanors, she would instantly throw herself into a semi-unconscious state and assume a blank stare that sent a thrill of horror through her parents. She became such an adept in this that not the slightest reproof was ever administered to her for fear she would throw herself into a condition from which she could not be aroused, for at no time could her parents by any methods bring her out of her "spells."

The case of Earnest Gunther is worthy of special notice in this respect. At the age of six he fell under the control of a stepfather whose idea of training children was based upon the doctrine of "Spare the rod and spoil the child." Little Earnest was consequently severely punished upon the slightest pretexts. He seemed to realize that his cries and manifest sufferings gave his stepfather the greatest satisfaction, and secretly resolved to forbear all manifestations of pain during punishment. He would say, "You can whip me, but I won't cry." And cry he certainly did not, no matter how severely he was whipped. It was not long before his parents began to entertain feelings of awe concerning his power of endurance, which seemed to delight the boy. He soon became an expert in controlling his feelings, and before he was ten years old he was entertaining his playmates by thrusting needles through his fingers and ears without betraying any evidence of pain. He was examined by physicians, who were at first under the impression that his early severe punishments had injured his nervous system; but they soon became convinced that his endurance of pain was entirely a matter of self-control. Unexpectedly needles were thrust into his skin at various points, and always with evidence of as acute sensation as is experienced by others; but whenever he was aware of the intention to test

him, he would "nerve himself up" and betray no
feeling whatever during the test. The boy was
unable to explain his action beyond the remark, "I
simply make myself so I can't feel it." His case is
an instance of the undeveloped human power to
voluntarily become insensible to pain.

### HAKIM ABDEL SUREDDIN.

A most remarkable illustration of the power of
self-hypnotism and the voluntary endurance of
injury without pain was lately given during the
author's clinic hour before the students and
members of the faculty of the National Medical
University. The subject was Hakim Abdel
Sureddin, otherwise known as Mr. Franz Cerney.
His object in presenting himself was to demonstrate
beyond the possibility of a doubt his remarkable
power to render himself insensible to pain. The
tests to which he was subjected were severe in
character and were convincing in results. Elsewhere in this book will be found illustrations taken
from photographs made during Mr. Cerney's exhibitions, and especial attention is called to the placid
countenance and the absence of all external evidence
of pain.

An account of the tests made at the clinic will
serve to show the degree to which this remarkable
power may be exercised, and may aid in demon-
strating the method by which it may be cultivated.
Mr. Cerney brought with him a large case of instruments, consisting of a series of long needles and

slender daggers with heavy handles, besides antiseptic solutions for thoroughly cleansing the instruments before their insertion. In every instance, before subjecting himself to tests, he desired to be informed as to the particular portion of the body to be experimented upon, so that he might easily render himself insensible, although it was not necessary to give him full particulars. In fact, it seemed to be merely a matter of convenience to him to know the locality to be tested, for when he was informed that tests were to be made without his knowing exactly where, he rendered himself just as insensible to pain, although seemingly with more effort.

When all was in readiness, Mr. Cerney removed his clothing to the waist and invited inspection of his body. The skin was remarkably soft and healthy looking, and pimples and blemishes were noticeably absent. There was nothing whatever to indicate anything unnatural, for a more perfect condition of the skin could not be desired. Here and there over the surface sharp-pointed needles were slightly and quickly thrust with instantaneous responsive signs of sensibility. There was positive evidence that no means had been resorted to for hardening the skin, and that there were no signs of disease of any kind. Manifestly, whatever unusual endurance he was about to exhibit must be entirely under his own control. When informed that tests were about to be made, Mr. Cerney drew himself up erect and resolutely, tightly closed his jaws, folded his arms, and assumed an expression of earnest thought. In a few minutes the surface of the body became rosy, and shortly afterward was covered with "goose pimples," which disappeared in a few moments, leaving the skin perfectly natural in appearance. He was then ready for the experiments.

The mouth was opened and rinsed with antiseptic solution and a large needle shoved through the cheek from within outward, without the least evidence of pain and without a drop of blood being visible. The other cheek was then pierced in the same manner, with the exception that a small quantity of blood oozed out through the perforation. The power to control the loss of blood was voluntary, and was demonstrated during other experiments.

The tongue was protruded and perforated directly in the center by a very large needle. Not the least tremor was noticeable and no blood flowed. When the extreme sensitiveness of the tongue is considered, as well as the fact that it contains innumerable small blood vessels, this test becomes remarkable.

The arm was uplifted and a bystander was requested to pierce it with the longest and largest of the needles, without regard to any attempt to avoid nerves or blood vessels. The needle was plunged fearlessly through the flesh, completely penetrating the muscles. There was no sign of discomfort, and not a drop of blood was visible.

The subject next requested that the muscles of the

chest should be pierced. He breathed heavily and slowly for several seconds, threw his chest forward, and assumed a peculiar expression, while the eyeballs seemed to protrude; the "goose flesh" appeared and disappeared, and he was ready for the test. A long, slender dagger was chosen and plunged into the muscles directly over the heart, and actually passed close to the ribs and made to protrude several inches from the point where it entered. No blood flowed, and no discomfort was shown.

Many tests of a similar character were made upon various parts of the body, with the same results. During each experiment the subject was perfectly conscious of all that was transpiring, and even entered into conversation and gave directions concerning the insertions of the needles. A trial was made to ascertain whether or not the anaesthesia was general or local, the test being to touch the front of the eyeball, as is done in ascertaining the degree of anaesthesia produced by chloroform or other anaesthetics before an operation. In this case the sensitiveness of the eye remained, thus showing that the anaesthesia produced was local, and directed at the will of the subject. All these experiments were of a very trying character, and occupied considerable time, at the expiration of which the subject was evidently greatly fatigued.

Hakim Abdel Sureddin (Mr. Franz Cerney) was born in Lahore, India, in 1865, his mother being a Bohemian and his father an East Indian. While a student in medicine he accidentally discovered his power to produce anaesthesia in his own body, and by practice developed it until he has reached the high degree of control which he is now able to manifest. The exhibition described was his first demonstration in America, although he has exhibited his remarkable powers before the heir apparent of Austria and other European nobility. He is at present having especially constructed a bed with iron spikes, which he proposes to have heated and upon which he will lie without the least discomfort. Mr. Cerney's neck is disfigured by several large scars which are the results of penetrations of the dagger over the region of the large blood vessels.

The wonderful power of self-anaesthesia which Mr. Cerney has so remarkably cultivated can doubtless be developed by a large majority of persons to a greater or less degree. It requires self-confidence and concentration of thought, together with a species of determination which can be better conceived than described.

# CHAPTER XXVIII.

## METHODS OF PRODUCING HYPNOSIS.

General directions—Objective method—Fascination—The candle method—Moutin's method—The Nancy method—Mes-
meric method—Exercise of will power—The rotary mirror
of Dr. Luy's method—The Hindoo sleep—Theory of the
Od and influence of magnets and currents.

Various methods of producing hypnosis have
been described and explained throughout this book.
Some of them are extremely simple, and can be
adopted by beginners with every chance of success,
while others are more difficult and are employed by
experts in overcoming refractory subjects. It is
always best for a student commencing the study and
practice of hypnotism to decide upon one of the
various methods that seems most natural and least
embarrassing to him, and practice upon that method
until a degree of perfection is reached. It is a good
plan to carry out all alone the movements to be
employed, as though practicing upon a real subject. This will give a familiarity with the method
of procedure which will be of great advantage when
attempting to work upon an actual subject. Nothing is more beneficial to a beginner in hypnotism

than to succeed upon his first attempt, and nothing is better calculated to make him succeed than self-confidence and familiarity with the methods of procedure.

### METHOD FIRST—OBJECTIVE METHOD.

Secure some unusual or bright object, several of which are described elsewhere, such as a disk with a bright or unusual center. Have the subject seated in a comfortable manner, his back to the light or window, the feet on the floor, the knees slightly separated, and the palms of the hands flat on the knees. Place yourself in such a position directly in front of him that your one knee will be between his and the other will be to his right. Have him hold the object in his right hand for five or ten minutes, and instruct him to stare steadily at it and to think of absolutely nothing but sleep. Impress upon him that he will soon become drowsy. Repeatedly assure him that he is becoming sleepy; that he looks sleepy, and that his eyes are getting heavy. Make these statements in a drawling and monotonous tone, with an expression of positiveness that admits of no doubt on his part. In five or ten minutes tell him he is too tired to hold the disk any longer; take it from him and hold it before his gaze for a minute or two, and then tell him to shut his eyes and go to sleep. Make a few passes over his head from the back forward, barely touching the head; tell him emphatically to go to sleep. Make a few passages from the back of the head to the knees, press the one hand, and at the same time with the other hand press your thumb between his eyes over the bridge of the nose.  He will be asleep by this time if you have with confidence carried out the method.

### METHOD SECOND—FASCINATION.

Stand directly in front of the subject, about five feet from him; have him stare at you blankly while you assume a fierce expression of determination; raise your hands and separate the fingers; gradually move your hands toward him, and then suddenly seize him by the shoulders and give him a slight but quick shove backward; rivet your eyes upon his in the greatest earnestness and intensity. If this method succeeds the subject will assume a peculiar and unmistakable expression of submission.

This same method may be carried out with the operator and subject in the sitting posture, as mentioned in method one, your hands resting upon his instead of being uplifted.  This is the old Puysegurian method, and is still employed by many expert hypnotists.

### METHOD THREE—THE CANDLE METHOD.

Have the subject stand erect, with the shoulders drawn well backward, the mouth slightly open, and the head inclined backward.  Hold a lighted candle about four feet from him and high enough above his head to make it somewhat of a strain for him to look at it, and instruct him to gaze fixedly at the candle for five minutes or more.  When you notice that his eyes are becoming weary, make a few passes from the back of his head downward over the spine, emphatically tell him to close his eyes and that he is becoming sleepy; continue the passes until sleep is produced.

### METHOD FOUR—MOUTIN'S METHOD.

Apply the hand between the subject's shoulder blades, with considerable pressure, for four or five minutes. If the subject realizes a sense of heat or cold, or experiences a tingling sensation, place the palms of the hands against his shoulder blades and press heavily for three or more minutes; then slowly relieve the pressure and withdraw the hand backward, when the subject will follow backward as if drawn by a magnet. Should the hands be again pressed against the should blades, the subject will display considerable discomfort. This method does not produce the profound stages of hypnosis. It may be used to secure the first degree, and passes then employed for the deepr stages.

### METHOD FIVE—THE NANCY METHOD.

Have the subject seated as in method one. Take a position about three feet from his left side, hold up two fingers of your right hand directly in front of his eyes, about ten inches from them. When signs of weariness appear, suggest in monotonous tones that he is going to sleep, and repeat such suggestions until hypnosis is produced.

### METHOD SIX—MESMERIC METHOD.

Place the subject restfully in a chair and assume

a position directly in front of him, either standing or sitting. Commence to make a series of passes with outstretched hands, the palms toward him. Let the passes be long from the top of his head to the abdomen, and always, before ascending to the head, separate the arms widely and rub the fingers as though throwing off some adherent substance; then let the hands ascend to the subject's head, always without actually touching his body. Continue this with tiresome and monotonous movements for some length of time, till the subject is evidently affected. If hypnosis has been produced, his arms may be lifted, and your command that they shall stay in position will be obeyed.

METHOD SEVEN—EXERCISE OF WILL POWER.

Seat yourself beside the subject and hold both his hands firmly but easily in your own; make a gentle pressure now and then, as though you were transmitting a flow of "nerve force" into him. Have him close his eyes and incline the head in an easy and languid position, and then commence the suggestions of drowsiness and sleep. Tell him he is getting more and more drowsy, that he is sleepy, that he is nodding, and finally command him to "Sleep." Ask him if he is asleep, and he will say "Yes." Make various suggestion to his mind, and he will be impressed by them as though they were realities. Tell him he is warm, and he will wipe the imaginary perspiration from his face; tell him he is cold, and he will perceptibly shiver. He is abso-

tutely under your mental control. Subjects hypnotized by this method lose all their personality
during the hypnosis, and are completely subject to
the slightest suggestions.

### METHOD EIGHT—THE ROTARY MIRROR.

This method of producing hypnosis is frequently
spoken of as Dr. Luy's method.  It consists in tiring
the optic nerve by gazing at a rotating series of
small mirrors, set in a manner to make them appear
like a mass of brilliant gems in motion.  By this
method a number of persons may be quickly hypnotized at one time by causing them to stand about the
table upon which is placed the mirrors, rapidly
revolving by clockwork.  As they gaze at the mirrors, hypnosis is produced.  It is surprising to notice
now quickly a large number of persons may be hypnotized by this method.  In social gatherings the
employment of this method will prove most entertaining.  Many who believe that it cannot possibly
affect them will be the first to succumb.

### METHOD NINE—THE HINDOO SLEEP.

This method is employed extensively by the
Fakirs of India to hypnotize their audiences, so as
to cause them to firmly believe they actually see
what is in reality simply suggested to them.  By
this process the Fakirs have secured a wonderful
reputation for performing marvelous sleight-of-hand
wonders which are in reality not performed at all,
but simply hypnotic imaginations.

It is best to dress in East India fashion. so as

to produce the air of mystery which is such an aid in this method. Sit tailor-fashion on the floor before your subject or audience, and then commence to slowly sway the upper part of our body in a rotary manner, without moving the body below the hips. Keep up this motion with monotonous regularity and gaze fixedly upon the persons you wish to hypnotize; utter no sound of any kind, although some soft and monotonous music may be played by another at a distance. The effect will be apparent in a short time, and in an audience many are sure to succumb. When they are hypnotized you may arise and proceed to exercise control over them in various ways.

### METHOD TEN—THEORY OF THE OD.

From very early times the magnet or loadstone has been employed as a curative agent in disease. Mesmer used it to a great extent, and other eminent investigators have made various experiments with its effects upon human beings. To Baron von Reichenbach, of Austria, belongs the credit of formulating the laws of what is now known as the "Od." By this term is designated the supposed peculiar force which, like the electric fluid, possesses various properties, and is given out by bodies under certain circumstances. One side of the body gives out a fluid different from that given out by the other side, and the balance of the two kinds of od in the body maintains natural conditions. When the balance is disturbed, great sensitiveness or even disease results. Or from another person or from some immaterial substance may affect a subject and produce hypnosis, somnambulism, catalepsy, etc. It is possible by passing a current of electricity through a subject to bring him into a state of rapport, so that he can realize the presence of only the one person who is traversed by a current in the same direction.

Hypnotize a subject by one of the methods given and set him back to back with a person suffering from some disease not organic, and place a magnet between them. The symptoms of the sick person will be manifested by the hypnotized subject. When a magnet is placed against the stomach of a hypnotized subject, the breathing will be visibly affected, and various other manifestations may be observed by using the magnet or the electric current during hypnosis.

In all experiments with the magnet, the greatest success will be obtained by employing the many precautions and aids elsewhere given for the production of hypnosis.

COSIMO is a specialty publisher of books and publications that inspire, inform and engage readers. Our mission is to offer unique books to niche audiences around the world.

COSIMO CLASSICS offers a collection of distinctive titles by the great authors and thinkers throughout the ages. At COSIMO CLASSICS timeless classics find a new life as affordable books, covering a variety of subjects including: *Biographies, Business, History, Mythology, Personal Development, Philosophy, Religion and Spirituality*, and much more!

COSIMO-on-DEMAND publishes books and publications for innovative authors, non-profit organizations and businesses. COSIMO-on-DEMAND specializes in bringing books back into print, publishing new books quickly and effectively, and making these publications available to readers around the world.

COSIMO REPORTS publishes public reports that affect your world: from global trends to the economy, and from health to geo-politics.